HOW TO S
LIFE WITH A
PROBLEM
DRINKER

A complete practical guide to
understanding the drinker in your life and
ways to improve your situation

Karenna Wilford

HOW TO SURVIVE LIFE WITH A PROBLEM DRINKER

www.karennawilford.co.uk

Published by Orange and Purple Publishing

Cover design by www.parker-smith.co.uk

ISBN: 978-0-9930702-0-4

Printed in the United KIngdom

Dedication

I dedicate this book to my parents who have given me so much support over the last few years and have always been there for me. I am so grateful that I have their friendship and that they have been so caring and giving. Thank you to my Mother for taking the time to help me with editing this book and for supporting the idea.

Contents

Section 4

Section 5

Introduction

This book provides knowledge about alcohol that will be the first step towards clarity, perspective and understanding of your situation. It is dedicated to partners and family members living with an alcohol dependant person.

Whether you are currently in a relationship with someone who is alcohol dependant or you used to be in a relationship and want more of an understanding on what happened and why, then this book will be helpful.

It is your responsibility how you interpret the suggestions in this book as everyone will bring their own experience and opinions to bear on what they read. This book is for those who cannot afford to see a professional therapist but it does not replace therapy and is not a substitute for professional help.

This book is about choices and making you aware that change is possible. It does not attempt to show you how to cure the person that is alcohol dependant or to establish what has caused the drinker to drink. I have not used the term alcoholic as in most people's minds this implies that the person is unable to change.

I hope that this book is easy to understand and will enable you to make any changes you want to make in your life. Whether there was initially a problem with drinking prior to your relationship starting or whether it developed subsequent to you meeting is irrelevant. People living in a relationship adversely affected by alcohol need support, whatever form the problems take and wherever they originated from. Throughout the book I have used the term "Partner" but this can also refer to a family member whether it be a son, daughter, mother or father. Throughout the book the gender of the drinker and partner has been avoided.

The book is divided into five sections:

Section 1 explores the history of alcohol and why we drink. It describes the influence of alcohol on the individual's mind and body, providing an understanding of the impact of long term drinking.

Section 2 looks at the result long term heavy or problem drinking can have on partners, families and society.

Section 3 contains interviews with people who have experienced living with a problem drinker. The names have been changed to avoid disclosure of the identities of their families. Each person has given their permission for me to share their interview in the hope of enabling others to realise that they are not alone and to know that it is possible to change what may feel like an impossible situation.

Section 4 explores options and takes you on a journey of self-reflection. The reader is encouraged to take what they wish from these suggestions and to use those most helpful in their particular situation. It details different strategies for helping you to decide how you can improve your situation and best deal with the heavy drinker in your life. Everyone has different needs, desires and dreams and whether you ultimately decide to leave or stay with your partner is a decision that only you can make. This section details the changes that can help you decide whether to stay with your drinker or not.

Section 5 details different strategies for moving forward, whether you decide to remain with your drinker or not.

I truly hope that you find this book helpful and that whatever you decide to do after reading it moves you forwards to a happier and more fulfilling life. I am always pleased to receive any thoughts or experiences people have had after reading the book and would welcome hearing your experiences by email via my website: www.karennawilford.co.uk.

I am passionate about giving people the tools and knowledge they need to improve their life and free them from any boundaries caused by circumstances that are perceived to be beyond their control. There is a great deal of information in this book and you may find it useful to re-read sections to remind yourself of why you have made certain decisions and to ensure that you carry them through. Knowledge is powerful only when it is put to good use. You will find some of the suggestions in this book easy to carry out and others not so easy. It is ultimately up to you as to how you decide to use them.

You may find it simple to read this book and discover parts of it that resonate with you but then decide to leave it to the future and put it away for another day. Life gets in the way, something else gets thrown at you and you decide that you are too busy or something else needs your time and attention. So this book makes it to the back of the drawer or has other things put on top of it and eventually becomes forgotten. It's up to you whether you allow that to happen or whether you are serious about making changes to your life that might initially mean you facing potential pain but will ultimately lead to a better future.

I wish you well and hope you find the book helpful.

Section 1

Chapter 1: The history of alcohol and why we drink

Alcohol has been used recreationally and medicinally, as well as been part of religious ceremonies, for thousands of years. Alcohol was made from fruit, grains and honey, producing wine, beer and mead respectively. The Old Testament and ancient Egyptian and Roman scriptures detail the use and consequences of alcohol throughout all layers of society.

We hear that modern life is stressful and that people have started to drink more alcohol but in the United Kingdom we drink less as a society now than during the 18th century. At that time gin was sold for a few pennies for a pint causing many to become addicted and for this time to become known as the "gin epidemic", The Government then implemented taxation on gin which produced a reduction in consumption. As a nation we are drinking less beer than we did 100 years ago whilst wine consumption increased after we joined the European Common Market and import duties were reduced.

The current UK Government has recently increased taxation and there has been much debate as to whether there should be a minimum unit price to dissuade people from over drinking. Many believe that alcohol use is similar to tobacco addiction and that increasing the price of alcohol will have little effect on those who are determined to drink.

Alcohol consumption in the United States was at its highest in the 19th century when the favoured drinks were whiskey and cider. Consumption has been higher throughout history when there was little clean water available and it was then considered safer and healthier to consume wine, mead or beer.

Why we drink alcohol

As children we inadvertently receive lessons from our parents or extended family about alcohol and when it is socially acceptable to drink. Children will see their parents celebrating with alcohol, using it for medicinal purposes such as a bad cold or for calming nerves, relaxing after a busy or bad day, after a stressful incident or argument, after an accident, to warm up in the winter, to cool down in the summer etc.

From our peers we learn that drinking is expected and required as part of the growing up experience. Most teenagers will at some point experiment with alcohol whether that is at a party or by having a tasting session of their parents drink cabinet. In films, television and literature, people's main form of socialising occurs around alcohol. Think of the number of television sitcoms that are centred on a group of people meeting in a bar or pub. Apart from smoking tobacco, alcohol is the main socially acceptable drug and therefore the side effects or eventual harm done by heavy drinking is also accepted by society.

It is recognised that in certain professions you are expected to socialise after work with colleagues or clients and that this involves drinking large amounts in order to relax, wind down from the stresses of the day or become more confident in a social situation. How do we know whether we are drowning our sorrows or celebrating an occasion or a good day? Like any substance alcohol is habit forming and an excuse to drink can always be found.

People tend to drink alcohol with an expectation of the effect it will have on them. If they believe it will make them less shy, more attractive, feel sexier or that they will get drunk easily then it will usually have that effect on them.

Alcohol is known for amplifying your moods - if someone is tired, they are likely to become more so and if they're in a bad mood it is likely to increase in intensity and become worse. Likewise a good mood can become even more accentuated. Alcohol is actually a depressant and can make people feel sad, anxious and depressed, causing them to cry. Those who say they are drinking to improve their mood may experience a lift and a high but then alcohol will have the opposite effect if they continue to drink.

The effects of alcohol will be determined by where and with whom the person is drinking. If they are drinking at a party they will feel differently to drinking with a meal at home. The situation in which you are drinking is likely to affect the mood of the drinker and make it more pronounced so someone drinking at, for example, a funeral or a wedding will usually react differently.

Alcohol has a reputation for causing fights and whilst some heavy drinkers can become angry, argumentative, aggressive and combative these reactions are largely due to social or personal circumstances rather than the alcohol consumption itself.

Chapter 2: The physical effects of alcohol

When someone has a drink the alcohol enters the blood stream by being absorbed by the stomach wall. The rate of absorption will be affected by whether the person has eaten recently, how much food they have in their stomach and what type of alcohol they have consumed. Having food in their stomach will slow down the rate at which alcohol is absorbed into the bloodstream and the peak level of blood alcohol will be reduced.

Any alcohol that is not absorbed will pass into the small intestines where it is more rapidly absorbed into the blood stream. Approximately 60% of the alcohol consumed will be absorbed from the small intestines.

When the alcohol has entered the bloodstream it can then access all parts of the body and soon affects the brain. Alcohol enters the nerve cells and causes them to slow down and become less active. By increasing the amount of alcohol the effects on the brain will be similar to having an anaesthetic.

The first areas that are affected are behaviours and conduct such as reasoning, self-control and judgement. We lose our inhibitions and insecurities, the things that we learnt to do later in life are the first things to be affected by alcohol. The first things that we learnt such as walking and speech are lost at a later stage and the motor centre, heart and lungs are the last things to be affected. As soon as alcohol reaches the brain it will begin to affect our behaviour even if we are unaware of it.

After consuming one to three units of alcohol the drinker may develop changes in facial skin colour, becoming more flushed as the heart speeds up. They can become more talkative, less inhibited and more confident.

After four to six units their sense of judgement and co-ordination will be impaired and they may experience some giddiness.

After seven to nine units our reaction time will be slower and the drinker's vision may be blurred and speech can become slurred.

After ten to fifteen units there may be loss of balance causing staggering and the drinker may have double vision.

After twenty units the skin becomes clammy, the pupils are dilated and there is little physical co-ordination.

After 30 units they could become unconscious. Once in a coma the drinker is near death and can die due to choking caused by vomit or due to unabsorbed alcohol in the stomach that can build up to a lethal point.

Drinking more than a daily average of 3 units for an adult male and 2 units for an adult female can increase the likelihood of serious diseases. Even a moderate drinker who has a drink before operating machinery or driving is going to have an increased possibility of causing damage to themselves or others.

How the body processes alcohol

The body takes an average of an hour to dispose of one unit of alcohol; this is based on a man weighing 150lbs as 15mgs will be burnt by the body every hour. This gives you a very easy way of remembering how long the body will take to burn the alcohol off. If someone started to drink at 6pm and stopped drinking at 10pm after consuming 10 units of alcohol then the body will have disposed of the alcohol within 10 hours of the final drink. This means that in theory it is safe for them to drive or operate machinery after 8.00am.

Approximately 90% of alcohol consumed by a drinker will be disposed of inside the body through oxidation or being burnt. Oxidation is how the body takes food dissolved in the blood and combines it with oxygen which then enables heat and energy to be released and used by the cells in the body.

Unlike most food that we eat, the calories generated by alcohol cannot be stored in the body for future use. When the calories from alcohol are being used by the body then the calories generated from fats and carbohydrates are stored by the body for future energy supply. This explains why heavy alcohol consumption will cause the drinker to gain weight.

Alcohol is mainly metabolised in the liver cells and the metabolic rate is fairly constant for each individual and will depend on weight and sex as this determines how much alcohol dehydrogenase enzyme you have in your liver. The liver can process approximately one unit of alcohol each hour and starts to process the alcohol about twenty minutes after the first drink is taken.

People think they are able to become sober more quickly by drinking coffee or having a shower but in reality only time will allow the liver to eliminate the alcohol. The stimulant effect from the caffeine in coffee will actually increase the rate that any drug is absorbed so any alcohol that is in the stomach will reach the blood stream faster. Some drinkers drink coffee to use caffeine to counteract the depressant effect of alcohol but they would have to drink excessive amounts to be successful.

Causing yourself to be sick does empty the stomach and help prevent you from becoming more drunk but it will not help the drinker to become more sober. Some heavy drinkers will use vomiting as a means of drinking more, particularly if they feel full of beer or cider.

Only about 2 to 10 % maximum of consumed alcohol is eliminated through breath, sweat or urine. Alcohol increases the heat loss from a body and the warmth that is felt after a drink is due to the heat leaving the body through the skin as the peripheral circulation is increased. If you were to give an elderly person an alcoholic drink in order to warm them up this could potentially be dangerous for them and increase the risk of them having hyperthermia.

Chapter 3: The effects of long term heavy drinking

Alcohol has different effects on people; it can be perceived as having "positive" effects such as relaxation, allowing them to feel more confident and outgoing in a social situation or being less inhibited sexually and able to express themselves. It can also have "negative" effects by making someone depressed, moody, angry and verbally or physically abusive.

Contrary to what many people believe, alcohol is not a stimulant, it is a depressant. Drinking too much can often lead to a tendency to violent behaviour, impaired judgement, slurring of speech, and short-term memory loss. The drinker will often be unable to remember an incident that occurred when they were drunk and will regain their memory of an incident the next time they become drunk.

Most people know that alcohol has a dehydrating effect, which is the main reason why excessive drinking can lead to a hangover. Alcohol also irritates the stomach and heavy drinking can cause sickness, nausea, and sometimes diarrhoea. It can also lead to temporary impotence in men.

The brain and central nervous system

Alcohol begins to affect the brain within 5 minutes of being swallowed. It acts as a sedative on the central nervous system and depresses the nerve cells in the brain, altering them and causing them to become dull. This affects the brains cells ability to respond to stimulation and large doses of alcohol can cause sleep, anaesthesia, respiratory failure, coma and even death.

The drinker's behaviour will be affected in terms of concentration, memory, co-ordination and judgement. The drinker can feel a reduction in inhibition and some euphoria as the alcohol impairs areas of the brain controlling behaviour and emotion. It can also cause emotional outbursts and huge mood swings.

The central nervous system can be affected by alcohol causing impaired vision and hearing and a reduced sensation of smell and taste. There can also be a loss of awareness of space and time. Motor skills will be affected, reaction times slower and the sensation of pain will be reduced. Sexual performance will be reduced so that men may not be able to have an erection and women take longer to achieve orgasm.

Long term serious drinking and dependency can result in serious mental disorders and permanent brain damage.

Bones

Alcohol reduces the body's capacity to absorb calcium and this can result in the bones becoming weaker and softer as well as brittle and thinner. Over a period of extended heavy drinking the drinker can develop osteoporosis.

Eyes and ears

A heavy drinker experiences distorted vision and finds it difficult to adjust to bright lights or sunlight. The eyes have a red appearance and the pupils are contracted and become like pin points.

Heart

Long periods of drinking can cause the heart muscles to become weaker and affects their ability to pump blood around the body. The heart can become enlarged and have an irregular heartbeat and abnormal heart sighs. Alcohol increases the risk of heart attack or strokes and increases blood pressure. The production of white and red blood cells is inhibited by alcohol.

Intestines

Alcohol reduces the intestines ability to be able to process nutrients and vitamins from eaten food which is why many alcohol dependent people experience malnutrition. They can experience a lack of appetite and may have nausea, diarrhoea, vomiting and sweating. With extended periods of excessive drinking the intestine can become inflamed and develop ulcers and cancer of the intestines and colon.

Liver

Chronic drinking can cause alcohol hepatitis and then cirrhosis. It reduces the liver's capacity to remove yellow pigment and causes the skin to appear yellow and can result in jaundice. Alcohol decreases production of blood clotting factors and may cause uncontrolled bleeding. Liver damage can cause fluid in extremities and fat can accumulate which can result in liver failure, coma and even death.

While rates of liver disease are falling in the rest of Europe they are rising in the UK. Liver disease used to mainly affect drinkers in middle age but now sufferers are getting younger. Up to one in three adults in the UK drinks enough alcohol to be at risk of developing alcohol-related liver disease.

Lungs

The drinker will have a lower resistance to infection and high amounts of alcohol consumed in a drinking session can cause the drinker to stop breathing and result in death.

Muscles

Muscles throughout the body will become weaker over time and be prone to atrophy, pain, spasms and feel tender.

Pancreas

A heavy drinker will have an increased risk of developing pancreatitis which is a chronic inflammation of the pancreas.

Reproductive system

Both men and women who are heavy drinkers will experience a reduction in their fertility and sex drive which can result in permanent impotence and infertility. Women can be at a higher risk of developing breast and ovarian cancers. Heavy drinking during pregnancy can increase the possibility of the baby being born with foetal alcohol syndromes which result in the baby having possible brain damage. The baby may have a smaller head with abnormal facial features and have reduced growth and development. They may also have poor muscle tone and speech and sleep disorders.

Stomach

Alcohol causes irritation of the lining to the stomach and can cause inflammation, peptic ulcers, bleeding lesions and ultimately cancer.

Throat

The lining of the oesophagus can be irritated and damaged from heavy drinking. The drinker can experience severe vomiting and have haemorrhaging pain and difficulty swallowing. Again, ultimately they can develop cancer.

Severe disease

Alcohol misuse is an important factor in a number of cancers, including liver cancer and mouth cancer, both of which are on the increase. Alcohol is second only to smoking as a risk factor for oral and digestive tract cancers.
Evidence suggests that this is because alcohol breaks down into a substance called acetaldehyde, which can bind to proteins in the mouth. This can trigger an inflammatory response from the body – in the most severe cases, cancerous cells can develop.

Chronic pancreatitis is another disease associated with heavy drinking. It is caused when the pancreas becomes inflamed and cells are damaged. Diabetes is a common side effect of chronic pancreatitis. There is evidence that heavy drinking can reduce the body's sensitivity to insulin which can trigger type 2 diabetes.

While studies suggesting that alcohol can help heart disease often hit the headlines, the reality is that the jury is still out on the extent of any benefits. And it is clear that any benefits which there may be are limited to very low levels of consumption – probably no more than 1 unit of alcohol per day.

Alcohol alters the brain's chemistry and increases the risk of depression. It is often associated with a range of mental health problems A recent British survey found that people suffering from anxiety or depression were twice as likely to be heavy or problem drinkers.

Extreme levels of drinking (defined as more than 30 units per day for several weeks) can occasionally cause 'psychosis', a severe mental illness where hallucinations and delusions of persecution develop. Psychotic symptoms can also occur when very heavy drinkers suddenly stop drinking and develop a condition known as 'delirium tremens'.

Chapter 4: How our reaction to alcohol is affected

How much a person is affected by alcohol will be determined by many factors, the obvious being weight and sex. Many people are unaware that women react very differently than men to alcohol and assume that this is simply due to weight.

Sex

Women have about 25% less alcohol dehydrogenase enzyme (ADH) in their stomachs than men and this leads to an increase in blood alcohol concentration (BAC). Women absorb alcohol faster than men and the effects of alcohol will last longer than in men.

A major factor in women's reaction to alcohol is that the amount of alcohol circulating in the women's blood will change throughout the month depending on where she is in her menstrual cycle. BAC's are highest during the pre-menstrual and ovulation times due to an increase in oestrogen levels that cause slower metabolism.

Many women taking the contraceptive pill are unaware that they will metabolise alcohol more slowly and therefore stay intoxicated for a longer period of time. This is due to an increase in oestrogen levels caused by the pill. Women who are taking the pill may find that they drink more as they are not feeling the effects as quickly.

Approximately 60% of women who have a serious drinking problem have been found to have started drinking after they were depressed. They started drinking in order to escape from reality and to stop them thinking about their problems.

A female problem drinker can have a higher possibility of high blood pressure, liver damage and stomach disorders and this is especially prevalent in young female drinkers. Women can also have an increased risk of brain damage at a lower level of alcohol intake than men.

Weight

Women generally do have lower body weights although they have a higher fat ratio and lower water ratio compared to men which makes women's BAC's higher as it is less diluted than that of men's. As an example if you compare a man and women weighing 150lbs, after consuming one unit of alcohol such as a small glass of wine, the man would have 15mgs BAC's and a women would have 18mgs.

This may not sound like a great deal but if the alcohol intake is increased to five units in an hour then the man will have a 75mgs BAC's and a woman would have 90mgs. Over a long period of drinking this would obviously make a large difference and for this reason women take less time to develop serious drinking problems than men. Men take eight to twelve years and women only take three years.

The statistics for the number of people gaining weight due to alcohol or developing health issues are alarming.

Age

The age of the person and how long they have been drinking will affect their reaction as an older person with experience of heavy drinking will become more tolerant to alcohol physically and psychologically and will be able to compensate so that the effects are not as visible to someone watching them.

Most people's tolerance of alcohol will decrease with age and for some that are on medication and have health problems such as diabetes or arthritis there are no suggested safe limits. They are likely to become more intoxicated and are less able to process alcohol without feeling the ill effects such as nausea and headaches.

Time

How long you spend drinking will also determine the effects of alcohol. If you have one unit an hour then a small effect maybe noticeable whereas if you drank 3 drinks within an hour the effect could be far more apparent. Taking more time to drink the same number of units will affect how much you are intoxicated but it will not change the long term effects of alcohol on your health. Men who drink more than seven units a day and women who drink more than five units a day are more likely to have a risk of cirrhosis of the liver.

Chapter 5: Types/Classification of drinkers

Historically people were categorised as alcoholic or non-alcoholic, it has now been recognised that the method of measuring needed to be more versatile and so the categories of light, moderate, heavy and dependant have been developed.

Light drinker

A light drinker is classified as low risk and continuing to drink at this level is deemed not to pose any threat to someone's health. This can include people who drink a small amount regularly, infrequently or those who were heavier drinkers and have reduced their intake. A light drinker would be someone who is drinking far less than the recommended intake.

Moderate drinker

A moderate drinker is classified as hazardous as it may result in harm if continued. This includes underage drinking as binge drinking when you are young that can become a habit. Studies have shown that those who drink a lot in their teens and early 20s are potentially twice as likely as light drinkers to be binge drinking 25 years later. Also included in this category are pregnant women and those who are carrying out activities that are ill advised after alcohol. It can also include binge drinkers if the binging has long time lapses between drinking sessions.

Heavy drinker

This is a pattern of regular heavy drinking that is likely to cause mental or physical health problems if continued for any length of time. This includes heavy and regular binge drinking. One of the definitions of binge drinking is drinking heavily in a short space of time to get drunk or feel the effects of alcohol. To be classed as 'bingeing' the amount of alcohol someone needs to drink in a session has been defined in the United Kingdom by the NHS and National Office of Statistics:

Men: drinking more than 8 units of alcohol equal to about three pints of strong beer. This is about double the daily unit guidelines of 3-4 units of alcohol which is equivalent to a pint and a half of 4% beer.

Women: drinking more than 6 units of alcohol, equivalent to two large glasses of wine. This is also about double the daily unit guidelines of 2-3 units of alcohol equivalent to a 175 ml glass of wine. The government currently advises that people who drink regularly on a daily basis or most days should not drink more than the daily unit guidelines. Binge drinking is most common among 16–24-year-olds, and is currently more common among men than women although in the last decade binge drinking among young British women has increased rapidly with the rise of the "Ladette" culture.

Binge drinking can affect the mood and memory and in the longer term can lead to serious mental health problems. It can lead to anti-social, aggressive and violent behaviour. Alcohol has been shown to be a factor in one in three sexual offences, one in three burglaries and one in two street crimes. Binge drinking has also been linked to self-harm and there is a higher risk of contracting a sexually transmitted illness during a binging session as people are often unaware of their actions and do not take precautions.

Dependant drinker

This is a regular pattern of heavy drinking carried out consistently and where the drinker has developed a tolerance to alcohol resulting in constant increase in alcohol intake. Alcohol takes over so that time is spent drinking or recovering from drinking; the drink comes first over and above anything else. The drinker experiences withdrawal symptoms if they cease drinking and this affects their partner and family. They could still be a functioning alcoholic and be holding down a job with sick leave after serious drinking bouts.

Alcohol dependency can result in a "Top up alcoholic" or a "Functioning alcoholic". This applies to someone who has a regular daily alcohol intake and continues to work, has a home life and carries out social duties. Whilst they may not appear to be drunk and are able to hold a conversation, they are actually consuming large amounts of alcohol. Their body has become accustomed to alcohol and it takes longer for them to become intoxicated.

When someone first starts to drink they may feel happy or giddy and if they drink too much it can cause them to vomit. After drinking large amounts on a regular basis it might take twice as much alcohol for the drinker to feel intoxicated and the "benefits" that they believe they receive from drinking.

When a drinker becomes more tolerant to the effects of alcohol it does not mean that there is less alcohol being absorbed by the body into the bloodstream or that they will have less damage to their body. They may develop problems such as memory blackouts as they continue to increase consumption. As a drinker becomes more tolerant they may feel that they are more in control of their drinking and realise that they feel better when they drink rather than when they stop drinking. Feeling worse when not drinking is caused by alcohol withdrawal symptoms and the drinker may drink even more to keep these at bay. This in turn leads to the withdrawal symptoms becoming worse and the cycle continues as the drinker continues to consume larger quantities in the belief that alcohol helps to relieve them. This ultimately leads to long term physical and psychological damage.

Alcohol dependency involves drinking about half a litre bottle of spirits or more a day over a period of several months. If the drinker decides to stop drinking then they may need help to do so without putting their health at risk. This can mean gradual reduction over a period of time or a formal detox under medical supervision. If a drinker has a relapse and starts to drink heavily again then they may start to experience pronounced withdrawal symptoms after only a few days drinking.

Signs of alcohol dependency

There are many signs of alcohol dependency that will depend on the individual's personality but be a clear change to those that know them well. They include the following:-

Smelling of alcohol, bloated face, redness to the cheeks and nose, bloodshot eyes, lack of eye contact, grey colouring around and under eyes, spider veins, slurred speech, pale skin colour, greasy hair and dry skin, musty smell, sweating, body odour or wearing very strong deodorant, unsteady in standing, giddy, disorientated, unable to sit quietly, large stomach, loss of weight, un-kept appearance, shaking or twitching, tearful, low self-esteem, tired and sleepy.

Some of the feelings that alcohol dependent people experience are:-

To be in denial and blame others, angry and resentful, indecisive, become secretive, feel self-loathing and guilty, unloved and lonely, anxious and emotional, scared and fearful, stressed and overwhelmed,
useless and judged, be depressed or on a high, confused and lack of concentration, unfocused and helpless.

Not all alcoholics are easily recognisable, the classic idea of a drunk is a "binge drinker" who consumes so much during a drinking session that they can barely stand up or speak coherently. This can be a daily event in extreme cases or be saved for the weekend as something looked forward to and then recovered from before going back to work on a Monday morning.

Heavy drinking often leads to work and family problems, which in turn can lead to isolation and depression. For heavy drinkers who drink daily and become dependent on alcohol, there can be withdrawal symptoms (nervousness, tremors, palpitations) which resemble severe anxiety, and may even cause phobias, such as a fear of going out.

Accidents and falls are common due to the effects of alcohol, affecting balance and co-ordination. They are also more likely to suffer head, hand and facial injuries.

Chapter 6: Social drinking patterns

Due to the recent economic downturn more people are choosing to drink at home. The pub industry has reported a decrease in the numbers and amount that people are drinking whilst the supermarkets report an increase in sales of alcohol. The Government periodically discusses raising the price of alcohol in order to reduce the rate of alcoholism.

Those who are known as "Locals" at the pub are very regular drinkers and known as social drinkers. There are equally many who drink at home either on their own, with a partner or with friends. These can be hard to distinguish as only those within the family unit will be aware of what is actually happening and even then it can remain hidden to a large extent. The drinker may know that they are drinking more than they should but manage to keep it concealed from their partner or family for some time. They may consume alcohol before coming home and their partner is unaware of this and only sees what is consumed in the home.

As drinking is a socially acceptable drug, drunken behaviour will often be tolerated and attributed to certain circumstances or even ignored and the drinker regarded as someone who lets their hair down after a few drinks. Family members may attempt to keep a drinking problem hidden due to guilt or shame, creating excuses for their partner's behaviour or even avoiding situations that may lead to heavy drinking. This can create a sense of loneliness and isolation.

A heavy drinker may be aware that they are drinking too much and make attempts to cut down on the amount they are drinking. If unsuccessful this will lead to disappointment for partners. Heavy drinkers are likely to reduce social, work or recreational activities to make time for drinking and recovery. They have little control over their consumption apart from when their circumstances dictate there is no more alcohol or they are physically incapable of consuming more.

Alcohol misuse is a major public health problem that places a heavy burden on society and affects a large number of individuals of all ages. More than one in 25 adults is dependent on alcohol and according to current Government figures the UK has one of the highest rates of binge drinking in Europe.

People who are in unhappy situations whether it be social, work or family- related are often prone to turn to drinking as a temporary solution for drowning their sorrows and making them feel as though they are coping by momentarily reducing the stress surrounding the situation. As a depressant alcohol will make them initially numb and then the negative feelings will re-emerge even more strongly once they have stopped drinking. This in turn leads to the drinker deciding to drink heavily again when they have the chance.

There has been substantial debate over recent years as to whether or not alcoholism is a disease. Many have argued that if it is classified as such then any form of substance abuse should be and even smoking could be called a disease. Some feel that the placing the label of disease on alcoholics insinuates that it is not possible for the alcoholic to control themselves and that they cannot take responsibility for their situation. Some believe that it is genetically inherited, others believe that there is a personality disorder or something lacking in the person's life

The facts and figures above give an indication of the real costs of alcohol abuse to society both in terms of policing and health implications and costs to the health system. GP's are aware of the continuing increase in people diagnosed with a drinking problem. They are being encouraged to discuss the situation with the drinker and the steps that can be taken to reduce their drinking.

This approach has had some success but the reality is that most drinkers will not be honest about their consumption either due to self-denial or because they don't want to be found out. They are probably well aware that they ought to reduce consumption but will come up with all kinds of excuses or reasons as to why this isn't really necessary. The drinker will find the most extraordinary reasons to drink and one of the main ones in their minds maybe their partner or family member.

Section 2

Chapter 7: The effects of alcohol on the Partner and family

In most cases where the heavy drinker is in a relationship the problem with alcohol commenced prior to the relationship starting which may not have been recognised or visible until the relationship was well developed.

Some people who find themselves living with a heavy drinker will question what causes their Partner's drinking to increase and whether they are to blame. The family's circumstances can certainly have an effect on the heavy drinker and cause a change in drinking patterns but these are not necessarily the cause.

As the partner of a heavy drinker your main concern will be their health and the effect that their drinking is having on you and the rest of the family. Our natural instincts are to ask the drinker why they are drinking so much and why they don't stop or reduce their intake. As children we naturally ask the question "why" on a very regular basis. Children are naturally inquisitive and ask the question because they want to know the answer. By the time we reach adulthood, if someone asks us "why" we've done something it will lead to a naturally defensive response. We will interpret the question as criticism and usually respond by becoming defensive, explaining our opinion as to why something has happened and apportioning blame to something or someone other than ourselves.

When a heavy drinker is asked why they drink they will become defensive, blame their situation or partner rather than take responsibility for their own behaviour. If you persist in asking why and become angry due to frustration caused by the lack of an explanation, then their response will also escalate and eventually either result in a full blown confrontation or provide the drinker with an excuse to leave the situation and have another drink.

Partners need support and understanding of what they have experienced with their drinker and also some guidance about what choices or options they have. They may have been going round in circles for years and feel their situation is hopeless. The feelings of anger, frustration, resentment, rejection and regrets combine to produce constant self-doubt and distrust of the drinker and the overall situation. These feelings can become all-consuming and lead to obsession as the partner is reluctant to discuss the situation with outsiders for fear of recrimination from the drinker. The partner can also fear that someone will tell them the problem is in their imagination and they are being unreasonable – after all this is what they are being told by the drinker.

Many partners increase their own consumption of alcohol as a way of coping with the situation. They drink to dull the pain, frustration and anger and this works for a while but like the heavy drinker, once they are sober the situation appears worse as they now berate themselves as well. A sense of self-loathing can develop and if they are also being told by the problem drinker that they are the one with the drink problem that they are useless, ugly, stupid etc. then they are more likely to believe it and eventually can become depressed.

Some partners develop problems with self-harming or even contemplate suicide. The stress of their situation may develop into physical symptoms that are then picked up on by friends, family or their GP. If they are feeling shame about their own drinking they are unlikely to honestly answer questions posed by their GP. Unless the partner wants to be found out and receive help then they are in a similar situation to the problem drinker. An attempted suicide is very often a call for help and the partner is so desperate to escape their situation that the desire for peace through death overrides concerns about the consequences and what will happen to their children or family.

Sometimes partners have no idea of how or where to get help. When in a downward spiral of protecting a heavy drinker from the outside world and concealing what is happening from friends and family then it is easy to get to the point where you feel that you may be exaggerating the problem. Some people lose all sense of what is normal both in terms of drinking behaviour and the consequences. You are so used to seeing a person drunk and your beliefs surrounding the reason why the drinker is drinking heavily maybe so firmly established that it is impossible to look at the situation objectively. If you have been told that you are partly the reason why the drinker is drinking then over time you may have subconsciously started to believe it. The next time you are told then it will reinforce this belief and so the circle develops into a downward spiral.

The family unit is formed to provide support and protection from the outside world and alcohol can have a negative impact on the family that has far reaching repercussions. If a family member is drinking to excess on a regular basis it will affect their own health as well as the mental and physical health of other family members. There are many forms of alcohol addiction or dependence which can make it difficult to detect or come to terms with by acknowledging that there may be a problem and that it has crossed the line of socially acceptable drinking.

People who claim that their behaviour whilst drunk wasn't within their control due to drunkenness are not accepting responsibility for themselves and their actions. There are concerns that labelling alcoholism as a disease allows this argument to be used and will not allow discussion or consideration of change and improvement.

A family member who has been verbally or physically abused will not necessarily care how the drunk is labelled but will want things to improve and for the drunk to become "well". There is often a regular pattern of aggressive behaviour that results in abuse that the drunk initially apologises for and promises will not occur again. Unfortunately with time this can become a more regular occurrence and eventually no apology will be given. Instead the partner may be told that it was their fault, that they said or did something wrong, that they deserved it or that the drunk wasn't responsible as it was the drink that was the cause.

Unless the drinker accepts that there is a problem with their drinking in the first place and wants to change then nothing will change. You can talk, shout, scream, physically hit, write, ask others to talk to them but nothing will change if they don't accept they have a problem and want to stop drinking as much or stop drinking altogether. This creates an enormous sense of frustration, anger and ultimately a feeling of powerlessness.

Heavy drinkers usually have completely different personalities when sober when they can be caring, sensitive and all the things that the partner originally fell in love with. They can equally be cranky, sullen and moody due to the alcohol withdrawal symptoms. It can be difficult for other family members to relax in the home as they are never sure what mood the drinker will be in and whether it is best to avoid contact with them.

Is my Partner a heavy/problem drinker?

Partners often feel that it will help if they know if the drinker is a dependant drinker or not. There are many signs of a heavy drinker and each person will have different drinking patterns and reactions to alcohol but here are a few examples of behaviour in no particular order:-

Change of character whilst under the influence of alcohol resulting in withdrawal and rejection of people close to them.

Change of character whilst under the influence of alcohol resulting in verbal or physical abuse.

An increase in the amount that they are drinking and the regularity of heavy drinking or binges.

Gradual decrease in self-esteem; not caring about their appearance in terms of what they wear or bad hygiene.

Signs of depression, either comfort eating or losing interest in food and general health. Lack of interest in activities other than those that enable them to drink.

Increased evasion of answering questions related to their whereabouts or the amount they have been drinking. (This may be due to a partner's aggressive questioning.)

Increase in amount of lying, deception, excuses for lateness or whereabouts. When the drinker is secretive and furtive as though they are hiding something.

Increased absence from the home or work for long periods during the day/evening or days in a row.

Finding concealed bottles or cans on a regular basis around the house or in the garden. (If the drinker takes out the rubbish then they may be concealing empty bottles or cans).

The drinker either smells of alcohol or uses heavy scents such as mints or cigarettes to disguise the smell of alcohol.

If you have to occasionally or regularly call work on their behalf to say they are ill when the drinker is recovering from a heavy drinking session.

If you find yourself making excuses for the drinkers behaviour and start avoiding social invitations or situations where they could become drunk.

When the drinker suffers repeated memory loss of their behaviour or incidents that occurred when they were drunk. This can relate to single conversations or be full blackouts where they have no memory of the entire drinking session.

Changes in their tolerance of alcohol, if they appear to drink little and become very drunk then they may have been drinking before arriving home. If they appear to consume large amounts before the alcohol starts to affect them then their bodies may have become accustomed to high levels of alcohol.

If you find yourself attempting to limit the amount of alcohol the drinker is consuming by consuming some yourself or hiding bottles. If you attempt to dilute the alcohol by adding water, tea etc. into the bottle of alcohol.

If the drinker attempts to disguise their consumption by topping up bottles with tea or soft drinks etc.

Consistent and increasing irrational behaviour in themselves and towards others, becoming more unreliable.

When the drinker repeatedly makes promises to change, cut down on their drinking and consistently fails to do so.

When the personality changes and rapid changes in mood swings become more severe, unpredictable and disruptive to the people close to the drinker.

When the partner regularly receives verbal abuse by text, phone or in person when the drinker is drunk.

The above list could be far longer as there are so many different types of behaviour but they are common signs that the drinker is more than a socially acceptable drinker. Often the partner will initially be in denial that there is a problem, once it has reached the stage that they have to accept there is a problem then it is very likely that other family members of friends will have already noticed the drinker's behaviour.

Whether the drinker is diagnosed as a heavy, dependant or an alcoholic doesn't really help the partner. What is important is that they are encouraged to believe and understand that they need to get help and they deserve to receive help and support.

Long term consequences of living with a heavy drinker

Many partners will suffer from long term effects of the pressure caused by living with an alcohol dependent partner. They may have panic attacks, severe anxiety, depression and develop phobias. Mental stress inevitably leads to physical problems such as high or low blood pressure and lack of sleep leading to exhaustion. They may feel fearful most of the time that something bad will happen to themselves or the drinker.

Drinking more as a partner is dangerous for your own mental and physical wellbeing. It is very unlikely to be successful in reducing the drinker's alcoholic intake and could result in the partner becoming dependant on alcohol themselves. As alcohol is a depressant they too can become depressed and suffer the after effects of heavy drinking.

If the partner was raised in a family where there was high alcohol consumption then they may regard that as normal and not initially be aware that a drinker has a problem. If there was alcoholism in the family or an abusive relationship then the partner will easily believe the drinker if they are told that it's their fault that the drinker is a heavy drinker.

The "reasons" a heavy drinker gives their partner for their drinking behaviour are often dramatic and unspecific:

I need some time on my own.

You never let me do what I want.

You're always nagging/going on at me.

You're always telling me what to do.

You're so cold and frigid.

You're useless and stupid.

You drive me to drink.

You keep questioning me and treating me like a criminal.

I'm not a drunk, I don't drink all day.

I'm not a drunk, I don't drink every day.

You're so demanding, I can never do anything right.

I have to do everything around here.

Everyone's always getting on at me.

Nobody respects me around here.

I work hard and I need some time to relax.

I can spend my money how I want.

You're just fat and lazy, I have to have a few drinks to go anywhere near you.

I never wanted to be with you.

You got pregnant and I never wanted a family.

It's your fault; I never drank before I met you.

Sexual problems

If you are living with a problem drinker then it is likely that you will be experiencing some type of sexual problems. If there is tension between you due to the drinking it will inevitably affect how close you are mentally and physically. If you find it hard to even be near the drinker because of the way they talk or treat you then having sex is the last thing you want. The drinker can retaliate with more verbal abuse and accusations that you are frigid, gay or having an affair.

You may find it difficult to be near the drinker because they smell of alcohol, cigarettes or body odour. Due to drink they can be clumsy and don't realise that they are groping, squeezing too hard or being rough. What is meant to be a playful bite or passionate kiss can end up being painful. If you complain or ask them to stop then the drinker may react aggressively and so some partners suffer in silence. The classic problem of 'drinkers droop' can affect a male drinkers sexual performance and either make them frustrated and verbally abuse or persist with fumbled attempts causing the experience to be prolonged.

Some partners find it devastatingly sad that when they first met their drinker they had a healthy and satisfying sex life and remembering how it used to be can make the situation feel even worse.

If the drinker is making disparaging comments before and during sex then it is very unlikely that you will be able to feel sexy or loving. Your self-esteem will continue to spiral further downwards and you may start to avoid sex which in turn leads to further verbal abuse from the drinker.

Those that do have sex to keep their partners quiet or because they fear physical abuse will endure the act and afterwards may feel as though they have prostituted themselves. They feel as though they've been used, that the act had nothing to do with the person they are and it was simply satisfying the drinkers sexual needs.

In some circumstances the drinker will use sex as a way of establishing confirmation that they are still in control of their partner. Others will have sex if they think there is a possibility that their partner may look elsewhere and have an affair.

Having sex with someone is ultimately giving yourself to someone and creates a deep feeling of intimacy. If it is enforced then the sense of emptiness, self-loathing or feeling of degradation is difficult for those who have not experienced it to understand.

Unfortunately it is common with binge drinkers who are out of the home for some lengths of time to find a casual sexual partner and not use contraception. The drinker then potentially passes sexually transmitted diseases onto their unsuspecting partner. A drinker will either deny having had sex or use it as a weapon against the partner claiming that it was their fault that they had gone elsewhere for sex because the partner is so frigid, unattractive, always nagging etc. This is incredibly damaging to the partner on a mental and physical level. Mentally it reinforces the belief that they are not good enough and do not deserve better or that they are in some way to blame for the drinkers behaviour.

A partner may have originally been attracted to the drinker because they appeared to be gentle, well mannered, and considerate. Many partners that I've spoken to felt that they were swept off their feet and had finally met the person that had all the qualities they wanted and needed. Some will have been looking for something that was the opposite to past experiences of their family upbringing or men/women they had previously been involved with. Most people I spoke to reported that there was a change in the drinker within a short space of time after the marriage had taken place. The drinker started to reveal traits that had previously been hidden although some reflected that because they were so "in love" or concentrating on the positive aspects of the drinkers personality they hadn't allowed themselves to notice a few telling signs that all was not as it seemed.

Many couples do manage to arrive at a point where the drinker gets to their rock bottom and agrees to undertake therapy or go to Alcoholics Anonymous (AA) meetings. As to what constitutes rock bottom, this will very much depend on each drinker. It could mean that they have lost their job, their home and are about to lose their husband/wife or it could be the discovery of health issues.

A partner can easily wait years for their drinker to get to rock bottom and change and the reality is that they may hit rock bottom tomorrow or never. I realise that this is not what you want to read and you are looking for answers but there are a number of things you can do and the third section of the book is where we start to look at the possibilities.

Some partners deal with the drinker's behaviour by ignoring it. They pretend to be asleep when the drinker comes to bed and will not complain or respond when they are shoved or spoken to. They find it easier to pretend that there isn't a problem rather than have to deal with the confrontation and ensuing arguments. The problem with holding back or denying there is a problem is that denial and internalising causes huge amounts of stress. The result is either an explosive release when things become too much or an unexpected trigger results in an unplanned reaction. You may stub your toe badly and the sudden pain releases the floodgates and you end up sobbing. Your child may drop something and the sound and shock catapults you into an angry response or reaction that would not have happened in normal circumstances.

Ultimately your health will suffer as when negative emotions are kept within the body this will eventually erupt into either stomach related problems, ulcers, headaches, lack of sleep and sleep deprivation leading to feeling that you cannot cope and finally turn into depression. Your health is paramount in keeping yourself and the family unit working together. It is far more likely that you will spend time worrying about others and most of all your drinker rather than yourself. Taking time to 'make time for you' is often hard but people who are constantly giving to other people physically or mentally are gradually draining themselves of a sense of self.

On the one hand it is important to form relationships that are mutually caring and loving and if a relationship is to really work then it has been said that you need to give 100% to the other person who you want to partner with, marry etc. The problem with this strategy is that we also need to recharge our own batteries or "refill your cup". You've undoubtedly heard about the glass or cup being half full or empty. Well people who give to others all the time are prone to allowing their glass to become empty and spending no time thinking about what they want or need. There is a balance between giving out and receiving love; if you are consistently giving out love and never receiving any then you will eventually have feelings of isolation and loneliness.

People renowned for constantly giving love, such as Mother Teresa, were receiving love from those people she worked with and nursed or helped. If you are constantly giving out love to a drinker who in turn rejects you or verbally or physically abuses you it is likely that eventually your sense of self-worth will be wounded. If you can think back to a time when you felt you were the person you believe you are and were receiving love this is one way of assessing where you are now. How different do you feel you are at present rather than how you were in the past?

Chapter 8: Terminology for Partners

Terminology used by therapists and doctors have described and discussed the Partners as being co-alcoholic, co-dependant, enabling and in denial. There is some confusion surrounding what these terms actually mean and there is a danger that they are too easily used in situations where the Partner is simply doing their best to create as much normality as possible within the home environment and their daily lives. It may be useful to look at each of these terms to gain a better understanding of their meanings.

Co-alcoholic

This term describes someone who experienced a childhood where they had an alcoholic parent and became used to the associated behaviours. They saw their other parent being verbally or physically abused and accepted it in order to be able to bear living in the household.

A parent may have been absent from the home due to death or divorce or be suffering from a disability or sickness that meant they couldn't function as a parent. The child took on the role of supporting the remaining parent and grew up too quickly, taking on the role of surrogate parent rather than gradually working their way through childhood to adulthood. In this situation the child ends up being very good at caring for others in the home and neglects their own needs and desires. The need for affection, love and security may have been unmet and the child learns that being helpful, needed and preoccupied with someone else's needs is the closest they get to the feelings of security that they want. They continue to help and help in order to drive away the sense of fear and insecurity in the hope of receiving love.

This pattern learned in childhood continues into adulthood and the person is often attracted to someone who they can help and who "needs" them. They are drawn towards people who need fixing or helping and are often in chaotic or harmful situations. The ups and downs can provide constant distraction from yourself and means they focus on the other person and their problems. Some people believe that you really have to suffer to experience "real" love. This is backed up by most of literature and the media. We listen to songs from all ages that bemoan the pain of love and films show the strong attraction and instant love rather than gradual love.

Some people are addicted to negative relationships and persist with relationships that do not benefit them in the hope that the person they are with will change once they have shown them where they are going wrong. They may be convinced that someone will love them in the way they want once they have their ideal job, live in a better neighbourhood, stop taking drugs or drinking. They hang onto the hope, remaining convinced that things will work out if they put a tremendous amount of energy into the other person. If they are used to a lack of love in their past relationships then they will be willing to hope, try harder to please and "look after" their partner in the belief that if they give them more love it will eventually be reciprocated. They may be terrified of being abandoned and will do whatever is necessary to keep the relationship going. They may take the blame and responsibility for anything that's "wrong" in the relationship and feel large amounts of guilt.

Being helpful to their partner can sometimes be a means of control and they do this in an attempt to give themselves a sense of security. They often have low self-esteem and do not believe that they have the right to be happy and that they have to work hard and suffer in order to deserve or experience some measure of happiness.

Our parent's relationship is a sub-conscious blueprint for our own relationships. We may sub-consciously look for a partner who mirrors the behaviour of the parent of the opposite sex. For instance the daughter of a dominating father may well form a relationship with someone who has familiar characteristics and take on her mother's role in their own relationship.

If you feel that it's possible that you may have co-alcoholic characteristics then please take a look through past relationships and assess whether this is the case. It is very easy to decide that you are not that bad and that someone you know is far worse than you, rather than really looking at your own situation and being honest with yourself. Are you someone who is more in touch with the dream of how you want your relationship to be rather than the reality?

Co-dependency

This term is most often associated with relating to women as they are historically the primary carer for the children and home. They are most likely to be caring and loving to the degree that they lose their sense of self. It is common for women who cease working in order to raise a child to experience a decrease in self-esteem once they are in the home environment on a full time basis. I realise that this may be seen as contentious and sexist and it is not intended to be. There are a growing number of men who now want to become the full time parent and in some cases if the woman has better paid work then it can become an economic necessity that the man takes on this role. Some would argue that in this situation the man will find it harder to retain a good level of self-esteem. Whether male or female, if you have been in a work environment, received recognition for any achievements in the work you have done and have earned your own income then it can be a huge change to not receive recognition from your partner for mopping the kitchen floor particularly well or changing 10 nappies during the day.

The rewards of being a parent are far more long term than we are used to in the work environment. Becoming dependant on a partner's income and having to ask for and in some cases justify requested money, can feel demoralising and demeaning. If the partner is a "fixer" or "helper" then it becomes very easy to start caring and looking after their partner if they are alcohol dependent. If the partner relies on the drinker's behaviour to determine whether they feel they have had a good or bad day then they may be said to be co-dependent. Some have said that being co-dependent is an addiction in itself, the feeling of wanting to be needed by the drinker and the belief that the drinker cannot survive without the partner who will ensure they don't harm themselves when they are drunk. They see themselves as responsible for the drinker and will not consider their own needs.

Someone who is co-dependent may well come from a family with alcohol dependency and where the associated behaviour of both the person who is alcohol dependent and others within the family is sub consciously what they perceive as being the norm. They are used to the chaos and unpredictability of that environment and unconsciously seek to recreate it by forming a relationship with an alcohol dependent person.

Enabling

Sometimes it is the partner who ensures that the drinker has a supply of alcohol as it makes their lives more bearable. The drinker is in a "better" mood and doesn't verbally abuse the partner as much and leaves them alone.

At the opposite end of the scale is what is known as "tough love" where the partner takes a strong stand against the drinker and makes sure they are not enabling in the hope that the drinker will reach rock bottom and then make changes to their behaviour. The partner is encouraged to concentrate on their own lives and cut themselves off from the alcoholic so that although they may live in the same home they mentally remove themselves for protection. This approach is encouraged by Al-anon and referred to as "detachment".

Using detachment can feel empowering for the partner as they feel they are able to actually do something and have some form of control over the situation and their own lives. In reality it can be difficult to follow through if there are children in the house as they may be adversely affected. If you let the drinker fall asleep where they have drunkenly landed or stop clearing up after them or cleaning them up after drink spillage or vomiting then it could be extremely disturbing for the children and have long term repercussions. As you cannot possibly predict how long the drinker will continue to drink heavily you could be waiting for many years for these strategies to have any impact and they may have none at all. Nobody likes to feel powerless and this is one of the main results of being a partner with a long term drinker.

The success of detachment relies upon the drinker becoming aware that they have a drinking problem and that they will want to change their behaviour by stopping or seeking help and treatment. Even if they do have treatment and complete the whole course or prescription there is no guarantee that they will remain "dry". The relapse rate in alcoholism is high and can cause further anxiety, stress and depression for the partner as they watch their drinker begin the downward spiral back into heavy drinking and all the associated behaviours.

The partner will still be in a position of waiting until the drinker changes their behaviour which means they may not look at their own needs and make decisions about what they would like from a positive relationship. The partner will need help and support before carrying out detachment in order that their own self-esteem is improved and they are able to like or love themselves rather than feeling high levels of shame and blame. A partner will often remain in a relationship with a drinker because they believe what the drinker has told them - that they are the reason why the drinker drinks. If they have been reduced to emotionally feeling they deserve no better, they are unlikely to have the courage and confidence to begin the process of change.

Some partners may feel there are no alternatives. If children are involved there may be a fear that they will have to remain and will consequently suffer under the control of the drinker. If friends and family have told them that it is their problem and they have put themselves in the situation so can deal with it themselves, then the sense of shame and lack of support will give them no incentive to leave. If they are financially dependent on the drinker then arranging alternative accommodation may not be possible.

Denial

Denial occurs when the problem drinker or their family refuse to acknowledge that the effects of alcohol are causing problems, whether they be mental or physical. They could be a combination of mental health, emotional, health issues, financial or social. Unless denial is recognised and addressed then the drinking problem will not change. It is essential in being able to make any decisions on the most effective form of treatment and for all involved to move forward and make positive changes.

Denial is common to all forms of addictive behaviour and for those outside the inner circle of the family it can be hard to understand. If you meet a friend or relative and ask how they are they will usually say that they are fine rather than give a true account of what is happening behind closed doors. It is difficult for anyone outside the situation to know there is a drinking problem unless they regularly see the drinker in a drunken state. Even when someone is seen drunk on social occasions they may deny that they have a problem and claim that they are simply letting their hair down and having a good time.

Even a GP can find it hard to determine a problem drinker as there is no test for determining whether a person is alcohol dependant or not. If a partner has symptoms of stress but says they are fine then a diagnosis will be distorted.

The longer someone has been in a relationship with a problem drinker and the more memories or ties they have with the drinker, the harder it will be for them to face the situation and come out of denial. It is far easier to put it out of their mind and continue with day to day life to avoid the pain of reality. If the heavy drinking is intermittent and there appear to be periods of time when the drinker returns to "normal" then the hope of change will be greater and the level of denial is also greater.

If the drinker was originally loving, caring and considerate before drinking became a problem then the partner will be hoping that they will return to their original personality and be more likely to forgive what has become unacceptable behaviour. Having children in the relationship makes it far harder to give any form of ultimatum such as leaving the relationship and the level of denial in this situation is likely to be far higher. The periods of little or no drinking can convince the partner that the drinking is caused by external factors or by the partner themselves. They can feel that they are the main causal factor and that if they change their own behaviour it will impact on the drinker's behaviour and solve the problem. They will find or make excuses for the drinker such as stress from work or a social situation.

If the partner finds their drinker is full of what appears to be genuine remorse after a heavy drinking session then they may well forgive the verbal or physical abuse that they received. If they hear promises that the drinkers behaviour will change and are told the "reason" why it occurred on that particular occasion they will be able to rationalise the negative behaviour and continue the cycle of denial, giving them hope that the drinker will change.

Chapter 9: The effects on children

Children in a household with a heavy drinker are bound to experience long term repercussions. There are many drinkers who genuinely believe that their drinking doesn't affect their children as long as the children do not see them drinking or the effects of drinking. If the drinker is not the main carer of the children they may believe that their children are unaware of their drinking. Because they come home late after the children are in bed, sleep off the effects of alcohol and get up after the children, then their drinking is not seen. If there is verbal or physical abuse then children are naturally far more likely to be aware and suffer as a consequence.

The fear associated with hearing the non-drinking parent receiving mental or physical abuse will remain within a child's memories and potentially affect their behaviour in adult life. Many who see the heavy drinking pattern will find themselves developing similar patterns in their adult life. If you hear a parent being beaten or are beaten yourself then you may enter a cycle of acceptance that, as the drinker says, you in some way deserved this treatment. External help is vital in being able to understand what patterns have formed and to be able to unravel the negative beliefs in order that more positive ones can be adopted, giving the child a chance to see life from another perspective and live a more balanced life.

A large number of heavy drinkers are deeply caring parents and are offended if it is suggested that they are harming their children. Denial may prevent them seeing the harm they are causing particularly if there is no verbal or physical abuse. Children may not see anything but they will sense the stress and resentment between their parents and know when something is wrong. They may see the evidence of drinking in terms of empty or hidden bottles/cans of alcohol.

In the worst cases children may suffer physical abuse from the drinking parent and be unable to gain help from an outsider as the drinking and abuse remain secret and hidden within the family.

There have been some cases in recent years relating to the church and children's homes that have highlighted the long term effects abuse has on children. What remains largely unknown is the scale of abuse within families which can go on for years and cause depression, self-abuse, suicide attempts and suicide in later years.

Children receive little or no support from the health sector, even if the alcohol problem becomes known. Interviewing and counselling children requires special training and many health services are reluctant to get involved. Even alcohol help groups pay little attention to the children and their needs. As with this book they tend to concentrate on the partner who might be in such a bad state themselves that they have little energy or mental reserves to deal with the children's problems as well as their own. Unfortunately in some cases the anger and frustration that the partner feels is due to the drinker can manifest itself in verbal or physical abuse of their children. The feeling of lack of control of the drinker can create a need to control the children and inflict mental and physical harm, whether that be constantly telling the children that they are stupid, ugly, useless or hitting and punishing them for minor incidents.

The other reaction can be to ignore the children as they simply don't have the energy to cope. If they feel they have failed as a partner and have low self-esteem that can easily be carried over into other relationships and within an unhappy household the children become part of the overall problem.

The children can also be overprotected. If a parent feels huge guilt surrounding the reasons why the drinker is drinking then they can smother the children with affection and attempt to hide the drinker's behaviour in order to counteract the negative effects of the drinker. The health of the drinker will obviously affect the partner's behaviour and if they are worried, depressed, anxious or tired they will not have the physical and emotional energy usually needed to deal with children.

If the children see the drinker's behaviour and the hurt caused to the partner then they will find it difficult to understand why the partner appears to suffer in silence and forgive the drinker. Some children may take the view that neither of their parents can be trusted and they will start to retreat into themselves. They can develop a mistrust of adults as a whole that will have far reaching consequences in all areas of their lives as they develop difficulties in forming any types of relationships.

"Normal" behaviour within an alcohol dependant household can involve anger, raised voices, lies and deceit and the normal family rituals of eating or spending time together and routines such as bath and bedtime stories can be rare or non-existent.

Abusive relationships

Anyone who has been in some form of verbal or physically abusive relationship will understand how the constant abuse insidiously eats into your reality of life; how you gradually become unrecognisable to those that know you well. If a child has years of abuse it can take many years to undo the damage caused. We all have an inbuilt system for survival that includes being able to rationalise what is happening to us in order that we can cope. Eventually an abused person will come to the conclusion that the way they are being treated is normal, bearable and be able to block the emotional or physical pain it causes. It is only through therapy or talking to a counsellor that the person may eventually understand that what they experienced was not normal and that they did not deserve to be treated badly.

There are many different symptoms of abuse that range from physical signs such as bruising or scarring to weight change, sadness, depression, poor sleep patterns, change in behaviour, stealing, lying, inappropriate sexual behaviour and mental or physical illness.

The children may often hear and see inappropriate behaviour by either parent in the home. The parent may confide things to the child that they wouldn't normally, due to the stress of the situation and in order to keep the secret within the family. Children will find different ways of coping with the situation by taking on different personas. The child may change a persona depending on the particular situation. For instance they may play the comic role in order to alleviate tension and then become the hero for the non-alcoholic parent, feeling that they have to watch and protect the parent from harm.

Some children will work hard to excel at school academically or in sport which will make people think there is nothing wrong with them when they are in fact crying out for help and attention. Others will develop anti-social tendencies and become embroiled in violence and thieving to give them a sense of power and control over their lives which they don't feel they have in the home environment. Other children will become very quiet and withdrawn, making few demands on their parents in an attempt to ensure they don't add worries or stress to their parents that could cause further abuse or increased drinking.

A parent that stays with a drinker "for the sake of the children" will routinely struggle with the question of whether the children are better off living in a complete family or a separated one. Separation and divorce always has a large impact on children but ultimately if abuse is present then they are likely to be better off once separation has taken place. There are often issues surrounding custody and access as a parent has to satisfy the Courts if they feel access should be denied or limited for the drinking parent. Depending on the age of the children and their understanding of what had been happening within the home, this will affect how they view and deal with the separation. If they are young and do not fully understand the reasons for the separation then they could very well blame themselves for the relationship breaking up.

Communication at a level appropriate for the child's age is crucial; it also needs to be done in a sensitive way that avoids destroying their relationship with the drinking parent. Whatever has occurred, the child is likely to want to have some form of relationship with the drinking parent. This can feel hurtful and even like a form of betrayal to the partner who is not alcohol dependent. Children are resilient but great care needs to be taken to protect them as much as possible during the breakup of the relationship. However difficult the break up and transition period may be, they are likely to be better off than in an abusive situation.

Parents may have fears that their children will develop a dependence on alcohol themselves due to the behaviour they have experienced and also due to inheritance of genetic tendencies. Research on the influence of genetics and the environment on alcoholic patterns are still being researched and there are many theories on this. Each situation and person is unique and needs to be assessed on their own merits. The most important thing a parent can do for their child is to create a secure and safe home environment where the child feels they can be a child, be honest, be heard and be loved. Developing a balanced view of alcohol and when it is appropriate to drink is something that is influenced by peer pressure, the media and the family. Alcohol is a socially accepted drug that has two very different faces and a child becoming an adult will encounter these and needs to have developed the internal tools to assist them in making healthy decisions.

If there has been abuse within the family it is essential to ask for help and ensure that the children receive an appropriate therapy or counselling. The main objective is to enable them to understand that what has taken place is not their fault, they are not responsible for the parent's drinking and they did not deserve the abusive behaviour they received.

Chapter 10: When drinking patterns change

Unfortunately it is quite common that by the time a drinker does eventually stop drinking the partner may have moved on and either realised that what they want from a relationship is unlikely to be fulfilled by the drinker or they have decided that they are unable to rebuild the trust and respect that was lost during the heavy drinking. Equally there are cases where the relationship does recover and can be resurrected. In these cases it is often beneficial for the partner to have some form of therapy in order to work through any feelings of resentment and anger towards the drinker.

In some cases the relationship relies on alcohol to keep the couple together. If there are sexual problems and a partner believes that having a few drinks, getting tipsy or even drunk is the only way they can become less inhibited or accept their partner going near them then this pattern can easily develop and become a habit that spills into other areas of the couple's lives.

There are also cases where if a partner is very controlling within the relationship then occasionally the drinker feels they have to express themselves, rebel or show that they are still an individual who can assert themselves. The drinking can take many forms, from becoming loud and abusive, being blatantly sexual and forcing themselves on other people or becoming so drunk they cannot function. In some cases this will unfortunately lead the controlling partner to reprimanding verbally or physically as punishment for the drunken behaviour. Again a cycle can develop that will not be broken until either of the partners realises that there is a negative spiral in motion.

A partner who is having an affair can encourage the drinker to drink as it ensures they are less alert and unlikely to detect any change in the unfaithful partner's behaviour.

The classic case where alcohol holds a couple together is when one develops an alcohol addiction and encourages the other to join them. This will ensure that there will be no reprimands or criticism of the drinker's behaviour and allows for mutual consent on how the couple interact socially or how secret the problem is kept. When one of the couple decides to change their behaviour due to health or other reasons then it places a large strain on the relationship. Resentment and anger can build up quickly if the partner who has reduced or stopped drinking attempts to change the other partner's drinking behaviour to match theirs.

Once there is a high level of anger, resentment or grief over the drinker then it can easily overshadow any improvement on their part. The partner can literally get to the point where they are blind with anger and distrust and it doesn't matter what the drinker does, it will always be wrong. If you decide that someone has a personality trait or habit that you don't like then you will naturally subconsciously look for things that they do or say that will reinforce your belief.

We all like to be right and this is the case in any type of relationship whether it's our partner, work colleague, family or friend. It takes a great deal of effort to change that mentality. First you have to be aware that it exists and then acknowledge what you are doing. Then you have to make the decision that you want to change and actively look for the positive things that a person does and says and practice stopping the negative thoughts and behaviours and encourage the positive ones. Sometimes we feel threatened by someone when they may make us feel less in control and we may be afraid that they will become better than us and so seek to ensure that we feel superior and remain "on top".

Human beings operate primarily out of fear and guilt. If we fear that something may happen that we perceive as detrimental to us then we will subconsciously do what is needed to allay that fear and reassure ourselves that we are safe from it. Where guilt is concerned we will do things that we don't necessarily want to do in order to satisfy other's needs and convince them that we are a "good person". We fundamentally care about what we perceive others think about us. There are those that are an exception to the rule but the majority of us will conform to basic social rules. As an example we may not particularly enjoy family social events but feel compelled to spend time around Christmas with in-laws that we have nothing in common with and would prefer to have at the most a few minutes conversation rather than an enforced day or more. This places huge strains on our balance of what we want versus what we feel we should do.

We all work on a pain or pleasure principle, doing what we can to experience as little pain and as much pleasure as possible. It is a well-known fact that the number of relationship break downs is highest in January immediately after the enforced "Christmas holiday season". It's a time when we are given social permission to eat and drink as much as we want in order to celebrate and have a good time. If someone becomes drunk and vocalises their thoughts and opinions then it can be put down to the alcohol and easily forgiven. A partner may want to leave the relationship but stays until after Christmas before announcing that they are leaving. The divorce application rate therefore rises dramatically in January.

There are also many cases of increased health issues as people hide away for a few days without being noticed and binge drink without interruption. For those that find socialising difficult or nerve wracking they can easily resort to alcohol. If someone has a severe speech impediment due to social nerves there is a transformation in their social skills after a few drinks until the point when they've had too much to drink and they start to slur their words and become unintelligible.

Many of us are far more fragile and vulnerable than we would like to admit or reveal to others. There can be an internal battle with past events that have shaped how we deal with current or future issues. Those that drink may feel that the only time they are connected and being the person that they believe they truly are is when they consume alcohol.

January is also the month that people realise how much they have spent during the Christmas period and the reality of their financial situation can be allayed with alcohol. So there always have been and always will be many "reasons", or some would say "excuses", to drink. We each have a choice as to how we will cope with what life throws in our direction and sometimes people are unaware of the choices and see themselves as powerless to change what is apparently happening or being "done" to them.

As someone living with an alcoholic you have a choice. In fact you have many choices and it is entirely up to you as to which direction you decide to take. If you carry on as you are then you will get the same result. If you make a decision to change something then it is essential to analyse the situation before and after the change. The result can then be measured and enable you to see and know what is providing the result that you want.

Many partners feel a great sense of guilt surrounding their problem drinker. When you are very close to a situation and feel totally overwhelmed it is easy to believe that you are in some way responsible particularly if your drinker tells you that you are. Is the sense of guilt so strong that you are immobilised and unable to become more objective and look at the situation? It is often hard to do so and having the courage to talk to someone and express your fears and concerns is the first step to being able to do this. The fear that you will be judged and maybe rejected by people can override the need to change. It can seem overwhelming and too much for you to deal with.

When you read the stories in Section 3 that are accounts of people who have been brave enough to contribute to this book, you may well have some empathy and see similarities to your own situation. I hope that this enables you to see that whilst each situation is unique you are in no way isolated from other people in our society. There is a great deal of pain and anguish that remains hidden and is not discussed. People seldom give a true account of how they are actually feeling when you say hello and ask them how they are. In many cases there is good reason for that as there is a time and place for the most personal discussions. What might happen if you avoid summoning the strength and courage to share the problem with someone you trust?

Section 3

Interviews

Reading the interviews you may well feel that your situation is not as "bad" and that there is no need to do anything about it. Unfortunately alcohol dependence does not normally stand still and stay at the same level; it usually becomes more severe with time. Our lives are not continuing along a straight line. Events happen and we make choices, at every moment of every day that will have an impact on our future. The decisions you make will either improve or worsen your life.

Denial is a natural form of self-protection. As the partner you yourself may have denied that your drinker has a drinking problem. Taking the time to stand back and seriously review your life is important and denial will eventually do a great deal of harm if you refuse to acknowledge the reality of your situation. It is often easier to be sympathetic and understanding of someone else's problems than to look at our own.

When I first decided to write this book I wanted to interview people who had successfully managed to stay with their drinking partner and make the relationship work. Unfortunately by the time I got round to interviewing the people I had asked to contribute, they had already separated from their drinking partner. This is not to say that all relationships where there is an alcohol dependant partner will end but it does tend to be the majority.

Many thanks to all of the people who were prepared to be interviewed for this section. Thank you for your time spent talking to me and your bravery in sharing past experiences and events that in some cases are still painful to recall.

Chapter 11: Amy

I got a job in the pub and met Richard when I worked there on my first shift. Richard and his mates had been going fishing but were rained off and had already been drinking before coming into the pub at lunchtime. I had just moved back to live with my parents after Polytechnic and didn't have many friends who lived nearby. I felt comfortable with him and he was easy to talk to. A few weeks later, after seeing him in the pub a few times, one of his friends told me that Richard liked me and I agreed to go out with him.

Out of all the other guys I had been out with he was the easiest to get on with and we had a good laugh. He would finish work and go to the pub every day, including Saturday and Sunday. I didn't really think about how much he drank and how often he drank. On one occasion we went to a party and Richard had come straight from work via the pub, he hadn't changed and was drunk. I had made a big effort to look nice for the party and was not happy when I saw him groping another woman but I brushed it off and didn't let it bother me as he seemed like a nice guy.

We met in November and 4 months later I became pregnant, despite using contraception and had to have an abortion. Richard and his sister were very supportive and he stayed with me for a few days while I was recovering as my parents didn't know.

A month later we decided to get a flat together. I had never lived with anyone and when we lived together it was no honeymoon. I ended up doing the cleaning, shopping, cooking, etc. although it was never discussed. He was never romantic and about a year later he was in the shower and I was outside talking to him when he said "We might as well get married". I felt quite chuffed that he had asked me as I felt he was too good looking for me and wasn't sure why he was interested in me. I knew he was going to do a second proposal but it wasn't romantic and I think he just felt it was his duty. He got down on one knee in front of friends, asked me again and gave me the ring. It was all for show and didn't mean much to me.

When we went on holiday abroad together for the first time I hardly saw Richard for the first 3 days. He went on a big drinking binge whilst I was left alone in the apartment. This upset me and I felt that I was being boring by not joining in with him but just accepted that was the way he was.

We had an engagement party but it was another three years before we got married. I was working as a waitress and he often surprised me by coming in to see me, I now realise he was keeping an eye on me. At the engagement party I was being friendly with a good male friend of mine and Richard got jealous, pushed me up against a wall and threatened me. Sometimes when we argued he would throw things at me, once he threw a glass ash tray which broke one of my teeth.

We were going to buy a studio flat and put down a deposit to reserve it, using my money. I suddenly panicked about settling down and was considering going travelling again. I didn't feel 100% about our relationship, but felt 100% sure about travelling. He gave me an ultimatum and said either you stay with me or we'll split up and you go travelling. I decided to go travelling despite my Dad and brother saying I should stay with him. Richard accepted the fact I was going to go travelling and we got back together after a few days.

Richard dropped me off at the airport and I cried as I was upset at leaving him. I went away for three months and I did miss him but really enjoyed myself. He collected me from the airport and it was as though we had never been apart. He had been living at my parents' house while I was away and apparently hadn't been working a lot from what other people said. I realised he had been spending a great deal of time at the pub, despite not having much money.

We moved into a rented property and didn't have the money for the wedding. I became pregnant again which pushed us into setting a date. My Mum helped me to arrange a budget wedding in

7 weeks and I lost the baby a few weeks before the wedding. To be honest, I wasn't that upset about it and felt it was meant to be.

Richard was gutted that I had lost the baby and supported me again. After we were married things went back to normal. As he was in the building trade it was normal for him to go for a drink after work every day. He didn't earn very much - his income was erratic and we always struggled financially. I think I had a low expectation of what being with a man was like. We have two children and he was a good Dad. Sometimes he changed nappies and would get up in the middle of the night to help with feeding the children when they were babies.

We had married in July and my Mum died the following January. It was a hard time in my life as my Mum died the day after I found out I was pregnant with my first son Ben. Shortly after my mum's funeral Richard complained that I had distanced myself from him. It wasn't surprising considering I was 6 weeks pregnant, worried about having another miscarriage and had just lost my mother. When I was in hospital going through the final stages of labour with Ben, Richard went for a walk. He had apparently fallen asleep in the TV room and came back into the delivery room at the last moment, missing all the worst parts of the labour. He went back to work the day after I got home from the hospital with Ben and I so wanted my Mum around and felt very alone - she had always wanted grandchildren.

My sister came a few days later for a short time but I felt very down. After Ben was born Richard went to the pub 'to wet the baby's head', it was an excuse to get drunk. Richard wasn't around much and still went out on a Sunday. I knew he was working but I didn't realise he was at the pub as well. I felt isolated and scared that I had to look after this child for the rest of its life.

When I became pregnant with John I think Richard thought it wasn't his child as we hadn't had sex regularly since Ben was born. Richard felt stressed at having to financially cope with another child. We started arguing and Richard wasn't as supportive with the second pregnancy.

Before John was born I had to work in the evenings, leaving home at 4.45pm. I would wait for Richard to come home - he must have finished work early at about 2pm and then spent time in the pub. I got so stressed waiting for him and was often late for work. I had a home birth and when John was born it was immediately obvious that Richard was the father.

If we had an argument he would snap very quickly and I had to shout back at him rather than letting him have a go at me. When John was 18 months old I needed to get an additional income and had to go out to meetings. Richard didn't like me going to meetings and was worried I was having an affair.

Once I realised he was in the pub rather than working I was so frustrated, I felt isolated and didn't feel I had any time to myself. He was spending about three hours a day in the pub and I really resented it. When the kids were younger he did play with them when he was around. I think I had hoped he would change once we had children. When Ben was 7 and John 5 years old, Richard stopped playing rough and tumble and wouldn't allow them to come and see us in bed on a Sunday morning.

Richard later admitted to me that this was when he started drinking in the mornings and more heavily throughout the day. I still don't know where or how. He's told me that he was trying to keep up with friends from the pub who were managing to run successful businesses.

I wanted to have a fresh start and we moved to an area with better schools for the boys. Richard always blamed me for wanting to move and I think he felt he'd lost some form of control. He had moved around a lot as a child and didn't like moving. He wanted to stay near his local pub and he didn't want to move after living in that area for about 20 years. In our relationship it was always me who made all the decisions and arrangements about where we lived, when and where we went on holiday, managing the finances etc. I now realise how easy I made life for him and how I took responsibility for everything.

When we moved the boys were 7 and 5 years old, I was 37 and Richard was 40. I was given money from my aunt as a gift and we used some of it to do the house up. I think Richard thought it took the pressure off him to work and he drank more. I don't know where the money went. Two years later the neighbours from hell drove us to move again to get away from them. I think their behaviour disguised what was happening with Richard. I wasn't aware of him drinking in the mornings or how much he was drinking.

When we decided to move, Richard took his brother to look at the house we were buying. They went to the pub and Richard was driving back in the van with ladders on top. He was drunk and drove up the bank on the side of the lane and the van flipped over upside down. He managed to climb out without a scratch on him. The police said that if the ladders hadn't been on top he would have died. The ambulance took him to hospital and when I arrived at the hospital there was a policeman next to his bed. Richard was crying and apologising, saying he didn't remember anything. The policeman told me he was well over the limit.

Richard was banned from driving for 2 ½ years and during that time I had to drop building materials off where he was working as he luckily had lots of work. He used a bicycle and told people he was cycling to keep fit. This was the second time he'd been caught drink driving and been banned. When I first knew him he didn't drive and I thought it was due to not having enough money for a car. He used to get taxis or I drove us around in my Dad's car. I eventually found out that he had been banned when I bought our first car from my savings. The insurance company asked questions and he told me he had been convicted for drink driving. After we had the car for about 6 months he wrote the car off and we were only insured for third party. After the accident he left the car, called me and we went back for the car which was en route from the pub to home. We lost the car and didn't have money for another one straight away.

We were a lot happier in the new house. I found the property, organised all the sale and purchase, did all the packing and unpacking – he did nothing.

A year later he started coughing up in the morning in the bathroom and said it was due to smoking but sometimes it sounded as though he was vomiting. Years later he admitted it was from drinking in the morning, it sometimes made him sick. I had no idea and thought it was to do with smoking.

I used to take the boys swimming on a Saturday morning and watch them. If Richard took them they told me he sat in the van. I realised later he was drinking in the van and then driving them home, he never liked me going in his van.

When Richard was 45 his father, who was an alcoholic, died of a stroke in Ireland. His father had been a violent alcoholic who had beaten Richard as a child. Richard was sad about his father's death, and I didn't understand why after the way he had been treated by him. During his childhood, his father had to be "dried out" in hospital a few times.

Richard had grown up in a pub which his parents owned and said that because he was a shy man he had started drinking to gain confidence socially. He also had a big complex about not being able to read and write properly as he was not often at school. He thought he wasn't intelligent as a consequence and had very low self-esteem.

We had to raise enough money for us to fly to Ireland for the funeral. His behaviour didn't change and he didn't appear to be affected by his father's death. He did stop smoking and I don't know whether his drinking was affected. He didn't go to the pub as much as he didn't know many people in the area. He drank 4 or 5 cans of lager each evening but I don't know what else he was drinking. If we were given a bottle of wine he always drank it. I once bought twelve bottles of wine for presents and although I hid them there were only two left by the time I went to give them to people. He drank daily but I didn't often see him drink - he wasn't a binge drinker.

Richard was never romantic and often called me "frigid" as I rarely initiated love making. There was no real passion in our relationship and sex was usually mechanical. I suppose I didn't really fancy him anymore and thought that our relationship was normal after having children.

I rarely saw or spoke to my friends and in some ways I felt isolated from them. A few of them had seen Richard's behaviour when he was drunk and had decided not to invite us to any social events. On one occasion things got very heated between a friend's husband and Richard during a meal. Another friend was chatted up by Richard at her party which I wasn't aware of until recently. At another friend's engagement party Richard upset a few of the people there in his drunken state which I found out about later.

We were struggling for money but hadn't been on holiday as a family for years so we decided to go on a cottage break over Christmas when Richard was 47. We drove there, it started to snow heavily and he drove well. We parked down the road and managed to get to the cottage. He started drinking and I took the boys sledging and walking, Richard stayed in the cottage most of the time. We decided to get snow chains to make sure we would be able to get home. In the morning he drove and I knew he had been drinking and I started to have a go at him in the car. We went to the shop and he started shouting and raving about his drinking, it was very embarrassing as everyone in the shop heard us. He calmed down and wanted to drive but I insisted, after telling him to get out of the car.

He cooked on Christmas Day but he was drunk, it could have been idyllic in the cottage. He was swaying and fell over and I was worried he was going to fall into the fire and was shouting at him. The boys watched TV and stayed out of his way. It was the first family holiday that he ruined because of his drinking. After Christmas he drove us home and seemed to be alright and more sober.

After that he hardly worked at all for the next two years and blamed the recession. I was talking to contacts and advertising for him to get him some work. He had enquiries and didn't get many of the jobs. I don't know whether that was because of his attitude or his pricing was too high. He sometimes worked with his brother but that died out and I later found out that it was because he wanted to drink on the job and became argumentative.

We lived on my salary and it was really tough. I can remember screaming at him to get work as I was so desperate. We had blazing rows because I was so frustrated that he wasn't doing anything to get work. He didn't seem to want to work and did nothing all day but cook the dinner. At this time he started drinking cider as he said it was cheaper. He started to become verbally abusive, calling me names and swearing at me in front of the boys. I would shout back at him once I became used to it and wasn't upset any more. Things got so bad financially that all our direct debits bounced and I had to ask my Dad for £30 to buy food for the week. It was a desperate time. Throughout the 20 years we were together, we sometimes had to borrow money from my Dad just to keep within our overdraft limit and survive.

Once or twice Ben, aged 14, told us to stop arguing. Richard was drinking and would deliberately pick arguments over silly things and it was as though he was just picking a fight.

The following year we had everyone over for Christmas. Richard cooked and got very drunk by late morning. Ben had a go at him in front of everyone for being drunk. Richard distanced himself from everyone and we got on with enjoying the day without him.

Six months later I was really unhappy with struggling and putting up with his drinking. Richard had no relationship with the boys and wasn't interested in them. He showed no affection towards me and I started thinking about the pros and cons of the relationship and I wrote them down. I was worried about the potential emotional damage to the boys with not having their father around and having to manage on my own financially. I soon realised he wasn't a good role model for boys and in hindsight wished I had left him years earlier. I went to the Citizens Advice Bureau for advice. They gave me a leaflet which I hid with my list of Pro's and Con's in one of my drawers.

Richard finally managed to get a job as caretaker in a local school but 2 months later I had a call from the school saying he hadn't turned up. I told them maybe his van hadn't started but was worried. I had to go to work and on the way saw his van. I stopped and saw he was sitting in the van. He had all the keys to open up the school, I asked him what was going on and if he had been drinking. He denied it but couldn't answer me as to why he wasn't at work. I was very angry as I was under so much pressure, working in two jobs and looking after the boys.

I drove off to work and the next day he was told he needed to go to a meeting with the Headmaster and Board of Governors. Richard told me that they had found out that he had been convicted of shoplifting when he was 14, and that was why he was sacked. I believed his story when he said that he had found lots of bottles in the caretaker's shed and said the old caretaker must have been an alcoholic. Over the years he said that about several people and I always believed his lies and deceit.

When he was looking for work my neighbours later told me that Richard would leave for work before me, hide around the corner and wait until I had left and then go straight back home.

Richard found the leaflet and list I had hidden four months later and he left them purposely on top of the bed where I could see them when I came home from work. He asked me about what I had written including 'I don't love Richard'. I told him I was thinking about things. He asked me if I wanted to divorce and I said I didn't know. I had never wanted to get divorced and was really sad and scared of the idea. Richard wanted me to say yes or no to a divorce but I didn't want to. I didn't want to be forced into it before I had really thought it through and was sure that I could survive financially. I also still believed that the boys needed their father. Richard made out that the boys and I were against him as he didn't think he was intelligent and was left out of conversations at the dinner table. One Sunday he stormed off swearing at us after the boys said he hadn't cooked the potatoes properly. Ben asked me why I stayed with Richard, I felt sad that he had said it about his own father and started crying. Ben came over and we hugged each other.

Things were so desperate and we were just trying to keep things together. Things calmed down again until the following weekend when Richard and I had a row. Richard dragged and pushed me out of the house, closed the door and locked me out. I urgently needed the toilet. John was so scared of what Richard would do and wouldn't let me into the house. Eventually he did and I was so upset because I had wet myself. Richard had got angry about us potentially splitting up. I wouldn't commit but I think he knew. He kept on wanting to talk about settling finances and said he wasn't going anywhere and I was the one who would have to move out of the house. I refused and said I wouldn't leave the boys or the house.

The neighbours told me later that at this time he was drinking more and regularly drove the van up the pavement. The locals were worried that he was going to run someone over. I had no idea this was going on.

Things calmed down until the next weekend when both boys were out and Richard started arguing with me about the house and money. We argued most days now, shouting and screaming at each other. This time, as nobody else was there he started pushing me around. He pushed me hard and I fell against a kitchen cupboard and ended up on the floor. He grabbed my shoulders and started hitting my head against the cupboard. I yelled at him to leave me alone. He dragged me to the door, pushed me outside and locked me out again. I walked around the house and luckily went in the back door. He wasn't hitting me as hard as he might. I think he wanted to scare me enough to leave the house. God knows what the neighbours thought. When the boys weren't there I thought we could talk things through, but no.

The same weekend he hit me against the kitchen cupboards and threatened to smash up my car. He walked round and picked up a hammer and went over to the car. I was pleading with him not to do it, he knows how much it means to me.

Sometimes in the evenings when I was working, Richard would forget to collect the boys and I would get a call from one of my sons in the middle of a meeting asking where their father was. He would be sitting at home drinking and I would have to collect them. I was running my own business part-time as well as working in a part-time job, and so was always out of the house working long hours. This meant that I wasn't fully aware of what Richard was doing at home and how much he was drinking. Work was my release from the reality of my home-life, as I threw myself into my business because it kept me positive and hopeful for a better future. In a way it was also denial of how bad things had got with Richard. He would constantly lie about how much he was drinking and then sometimes when he was particularly depressed he would admit he was an alcoholic. Ironically I would immediately tell him he wasn't one! Sadly, I didn't realise the effect Richard's behaviour was having on our sons, especially as I wasn't at home much. At that time I felt my sons' and I were just surviving.

Richard managed to get a cleaning job and things calmed down. He still drank a lot of cider but managed to do a few hours' work in the evening. On the third day of his new job he phoned me up and said he'd had a row with his supervisor and had been told he wasn't doing his work properly. I told him to calm down and reasoned with him that we needed the money. He put the phone down and drove back home after he was sacked. When he got back home, he told me that when he had parked the car at work someone had knocked off his wing mirror and damaged the front of the car. He took me out, showed me the damage and I believed him. When we went inside we started rowing. A few minutes later the police knocked on the door and arrested Richard for drink driving and he was taken away. Ben said to me "He'll never learn, will he Mum?" Richard was convicted, fined and banned for 4 years. It was his third conviction and he could have gone to prison.

Once we had agreed to get divorced he tried to pull the rings off my finger, saying I didn't need them anymore. He had to get Vaseline to get them off and he took them. He said he threw them in the river but I am sure he pawned them to buy drink. After wearing rings for 16 years I was very conscious of not wearing them from this time onwards. I walked around the house with my wallet and keys on me because he was constantly stealing money out of my purse and I wanted the keys in case he dragged me out of the house and locked me out again.

We were both smoking at this time and he was always asking me for cigarettes and followed me about every time I had one. He kept asking where I was going and accused me of having an affair. He kept disappearing, saying he was going to a meeting but I knew he was in his van drinking.

He kept talking about his childhood and upbringing, blaming his behaviour on that. His father used to beat him, his mother didn't care about him and he caught her in bed with another man. I suggested he see a counsellor and talk to someone. He said that is what a wife was for. He said he was depressed and that he had been to the doctor who advised that he shouldn't stop drinking

Immediately, but should cut down. I don't think he went to the doctor at all.

A local churchgoer tried to help Richard and get him involved in the church. He was invited to various events to try and get him off the drink. He used to try and control me and then started to play the victim. He became more depressed when he knew I was serious about divorcing him. A neighbour tried to take him to AA and picked him up and took him there. He asked Richard to go another time but he didn't bother going.

Before Christmas Richard was drinking all day, everyday. He just sat in the lounge watching TV and drank. If he needed to go to the toilet he opened the patio doors and urinated right outside rather than walk to the toilet. I kept finding half full glasses and some empty bottles of cider. He wasn't working and I don't know what time he started drinking as I went out to work. He would often fall asleep on the sofa and would then come to bed. Even though we were divorcing he still wanted to have sex which I refused. We slept in the same bed because there was no choice but I didn't want any physical contact.

I went out for a pre-Christmas dinner with work colleagues and had a nice time. When I got back Richard was snoring so I went and slept in the lounge on the sofa. I was woken by Richard coming in and switching the light on. He asked me what I was doing there and I told him he'd been snoring and to leave me alone. He switched the light off and left but five minutes later he came back and switched the light on again. Eventually I got back to sleep but was woken up by Richard punching me in the head. I was crying and screaming at him to leave me alone and he did. I know he could have hit me harder which scared me. He left the room and I went and slept on the floor in the children's bedroom where I felt most safe.

This was the lowest point as I was so scared. I called my sister the next morning as I didn't know what to do. She told me to go to the police so I went to the police and they said they would arrest him and keep him overnight but would have to release him again. I was warned about the repercussions so didn't make a formal statement but was advised that it was on record so if anything else happened it would be taken into account.

We were planning to go to my sister for Christmas but Richard wasn't invited. The following day he asked me to drop him off at the doctor, although he asked me to leave him outside a supermarket that had cheap cider. In the car I asked him why he had hit me on the head. He denied it first of all and when I asked why my head still hurt, he said any man would have done it and that I deserved it. As I knew where he was I decided to leave a day earlier for my sister's and left quickly while Richard was out. We loaded the car with what we needed and anything of value that Richard might be able to pawn.

As soon as we left and were driving, the kids were laughing and joking as we all relaxed. It was the first time we had done that for months as it had been so stressful. We had a lovely Christmas and my sister offered to pay for a solicitor for me to get a divorce. Sadly Richard was left on his own at home that Christmas and while we were away he called the kids to ask how to use the freeview box but didn't wish them a happy Christmas. They were disappointed that Richard didn't call back after they left him a message. I was worried about what the condition the house would be in when we got back. I walked into the lounge and Richard didn't say anything to me when I said hello. He was acting as if we had never been away.

It was awful being back and I felt as though I was walking on eggshells. He flared up at the least excuse. The boys and I lived in the bedrooms as Richard was always in the lounge. He threatened to hit me several times and if he walked past me he would bump into me deliberately. He said I should leave the house and he should stay but he didn't discuss the boys. The only time he really talked to me was when he wanted to discuss the house or he wanted some money. He followed me around the house saying he wanted to do something in the room I was in. He constantly abused me verbally, swearing at me and the boys. It didn't matter how I behaved towards him – whether I was nice to him, ignored him or was nasty to him, he still behaved the same way and I never knew when he would get angry and violent. Once, I made him some sandwiches, gave him the best part of the bread and he still had a go at me for giving him awful food, and threw them in the bin!

I was living and working in the bedroom and was fed up with it and I went into the lounge. I changed the TV channel over to watch a programme that I wanted to watch and Richard started arguing. Ben came in and Richard slapped me in the face in front of Ben. Ben was very mature, stayed calm and tried to calm Richard down. Richard started having a go at Ben and followed him into the kitchen and cornered him. Ben was so scared that he picked up a knife and threatened Richard. I told Ben to put the knife down which he did. Richard was really angry but stayed quiet which was worrying. Ben left the kitchen and went to his room and Richard followed him, went into their room and shoved Ben. Ben told Richard that he had ruined his life and that he had been thinking about running away but hadn't because of me. I was shocked as I hadn't realised the children had been affected so badly. Richard left the room and went back to the lounge.

This was a turning point and I decided we should pack up and go to my Dad's. We quickly packed up and left. Richard was in the lounge watching TV and didn't hear us leaving the house. I had often seen John who was 14 years, hiding under his duvet in his bedroom where he felt safest and 16 year old Ben had eczema that had got really bad due to all the stress.

We came back home the next evening and Richard didn't say anything. I think he was hoping we would want to leave and then he would have the house. The next day I took Ben with me to the police to make a statement and the police decided to arrest

Richard. The police said they would call me in advance to warn me it was about to happen. They had to make sure they had a strong case before arresting him which they did a couple of days later when I was at work and the boys were at school.

Richard was in the cells and was banging on the door saying he was worried about his heart. They took him to hospital and realised he had been drinking and kept him for five days to dry him out. We were told he wouldn't be coming home for five days and it was such a relief for us all and was as though we were on holiday. When he was in hospital his sister-in-law called me and said she had visited him and that he had said he was sorry and was going to change.

When Richard was interviewed he admitted to slapping me and pleaded guilty. He was bailed but not allowed to come back to the house. His brother picked him up and got him into a hotel for a couple of nights. His family wouldn't take him in and couldn't afford the hotel, so they arranged for him to go to a homeless shelter. His sister came to collect his clothes and I think she thought I would take him back home. I knew that his family wanted me to look after him.

Richard wasn't meant to contact me but he left me a message saying could he have the tent as he was homeless and it was snowing. I had been assigned a counsellor through Women's Support Services. I called her and told her that I felt dreadful and she told me that he was trying to get me to change my mind and make me feel guilty. It was really tough to deal with. I was sure his family would take him in and spoke to his sister and said he needed support from his family. We ended up having a row and I put the phone down.

He turned up at the house a couple of weeks later on a Sunday night at 11.30pm. I heard someone walking up to the front door and he was banging on the door asking me to let him in. He walked around to the back of the house to see if he could get in, I was really scared and called the police who came and arrested him for breaking his bail conditions.

He went to court and was told to stay away from me and the house. A few weeks later I came out of the house, was going towards the car and saw him by the side of the house, sitting with a bottle of cider. He asked me why I was doing this to him, I said nothing and he said he might as well commit suicide. My counsellor had warned me that he might say that and I was prepared. I said 'You're just trying to play with my emotions' and then told him I would phone his brother to come and pick him up. I got in the car and drove off as I had to pick Ben up. I called John who was in the house and warned him Richard was there and not to let him in. Richard banged on the window of John's bedroom telling him to let him in.

I collected Ben and got back into the house and called the police who came and arrested Richard. Because he had broken bail again he was sent to prison for three weeks. It was a relief to know that he was warm and being fed and we wouldn't be bothered by him anymore. He was convicted and got a restraining order which also stopped his family contacting me as well.

I had great support from friends, family and the police which helped a lot. The boys don't want to see him. The Social Worker said they were very mature and well-grounded despite what had happened to them. I stayed with Richard for a long time because of the boys and have often wondered what would have happened if I had carried on living with him. The neighbours, who were a wonderful support to me in the last couple of months, said that they feared for our lives because they heard the arguments, shouting and screaming. It's really sad how the boys feel about him as they don't even want to speak about Richard.

I have learnt that I was too trusting and could not see what was going on. I believed Richard's lies and became submissive. I thought it was normal behaviour to be treated the way he treated me. My boys have always been the most important part of my life and I realise it even more now. They have been rocks and so supportive.

They have been amazing. I've always believed I was strong but now I realise how much Richard had controlled me.

I regret losing contact with some of my friends because of Richard's behaviour. They have now told me some of the things he did. I realise how important my friends are and how much they mean to me.

Because of our financial difficulties over the years, we haven't had a proper family holiday for over 7 years. I deeply regret not giving my sons happy memories of many wonderful family holidays and so this coming Christmas we are going on a holiday of a lifetime to a country the other side of the world. I feel it is the last chance we will have to spend a memorable holiday together before my 16 and 18 year old sons are too old to want to go on holiday with me. My part-time business has financed the holiday and we are all so excited about it. Life has amazing twists and turns.

My advice to you is that you have to think of what is best for you and any children. You need to have a serious think and write down how you feel about your partner, write down all the pros and cons. You only have one life and you deserve to be treated well. You shouldn't allow yourself to be treated badly.

Open your eyes as to what your partner may be hiding as they can be very devious. Try and persuade them to get help and if they don't want to, know then that you have to move on. Don't accept it if someone says they will change and don't stay with them unless they show proof that they have changed.

Don't worry about what other people think of you. You have got to be strong and do what you want. Focus on yourself and what outcome you want. Use your friends and family for support as you'll need it, it's a team effort! In the last few months I felt that I was in a protective bubble with the support structure around me – no matter what Richard did to me. Seek professional advice from a solicitor, counsellor or therapist.

Now I feel completely free and back to the bubbly, happy, fun-loving person I used to be before I met Richard. I feel really positive about future relationships as it is about 18 months since Richard left our home and many years since I truly had feelings for him. I know what I want in a relationship now and it will be the complete opposite to what I had with Richard. I think when you are young you just fall into things. I have written a list of the qualities I would like to have in a future partner.

I now realise that I made a bad choice when I met Richard but will never regret my 20 year relationship with him because I have been given 2 wonderful sons. I only regret the length of time I stayed with him and what my sons experienced and suffered. Both my sons are supportive of me dating and I have recently been in a relationship with a lovely caring man. This has really opened my eyes to the fact that there are some wonderful and kind men who I can trust and who will treat me with respect. The experiences I have had in this recent relationship are so refreshing for me and a wonderful part of my new life. They say life begins at 40 and for me my life has just begun at 47!

Chapter 12: Chris

When I left university I had a job in London and lived with my friend Mike who was manager of an off-licence. I met Jane in the off-licence when she came in as a customer and occasionally met up with Jane and her family in the pub. I socialised a lot with her family and went to family events which involved almost everyone drinking a lot. I started to drink more when I was living above the off-license but did not drink to the point where I was causing problems for myself or others.

There was a gradual attraction between Jane and me but we fell out a few times when she was drunk. We were never actually a couple but tended to meet in a group as friends, there were periods when we became closer but it never really went anywhere.

Jane met another guy and had a baby she called Paul. When Paul was 1 years old we went out on a date. I later found out this was to make Paul's father jealous and we fell out over that.

I moved to Surrey and she moved to South London where she became very lonely and one of her brothers persuaded me to go and see her. I started seeing her regularly and was probably the only friend she was seeing. We became a couple at that point when Paul was about 3 years old. We lived together for half the time until I moved in with her about a year later.

There were occasions when she got quite drunk and she drank regularly. She had a group of friends who were heavy drinkers and who weren't a good influence but her drinking wasn't a big problem at that time.

Paul was 5 when our daughter Lisa was born. Jane had drunk relatively little when she was pregnant but after the baby was born she said she had post natal depression and also started to drink heavily, I'm not sure what was causing the depression. It quickly became apparent that her friends weren't being helpful as they became drinking partners.

I had to go to Scotland for work but it was cancelled at the last minute and I came home at 7p.m. As I got out of my car and walked towards the house I could hear a terrified child screaming. As I got closer to the door I realised it was coming from inside our house, I found Lisa alone in the house in her cot in the dark. She was standing up holding her arms out towards the door, screaming like I never heard before. I picked her up and after about 30 minutes she started to calm down but was still clinging to me with strength that belied her tiny size and she was shaking all the time.

Jane had taken Paul to a friend's house and was having a major drinking session. I don't know how long Lisa had been alone and I've never forgiven Jane for that. I still had to go to Scotland for work and persuaded my friend Mike to go round and keep an eye on things.

On another occasion she went out clubbing and came back very drunk long after it had closed. She was drinking heavily on a regular basis and things got bad. She stopped getting up to deal with the kids and I fed them and took Paul to school, leaving Lisa with Jane when I went to work.

We intended to move and I made this happen quickly in order to get her away from the group of friends. Paul was 6 when we moved, we had little money, she stopped drinking and there was little social drinking. About a year later she started to disappear to friends' houses to drink and came back drunk. To start with she took the children with her but after a couple of years she arranged to leave them with someone and then go drinking. I would come home and find notes about where the kids were and have to go and find them to bring them home.

When Lisa was about 2 years old Jane had gone to see a friend and taken the kids with her. When she came back very drunk late afternoon she left her keys and said she was going out. She came back at 2am very drunk and it became a regular pattern, on or around the twentieth day of her monthly cycle she would disappear and reappear drunk in the early hours.

There was a lot of friction between us. She would promise it wouldn't happen again and when she did go out promised to be back at 11pm but she never was. There was some drinking going on during the day but once Lisa was 4 and went to school, Jane started drinking more and sometimes when I got back home at 6.30pm she was drunk.

When she was drunk she was unpredictable as she had mood swings and was quite aggressive. Long before Paul was born she had been depressed and was prescribed Valium by a doctor. When the doctor weaned her off she changed doctors. I don't know how much the mood swings were to do with the Valium but it made her become drunk very quickly.

She started to drink uncontrollably and if she went to the pub wouldn't leave until it closed. Then she would go to a club or a friend's house and continue drinking, coming home at 3am or later.

If she went to friends or was at home she drank until there was nothing left. This became daily once she got a part-time job and had money to spend on drink. Her drinking affected the children as she lost her temper with them very easily and was very erratic. When she was drinking she didn't think about their safety, she would leave the hot iron on the ironing board. It stopped the children having friends round. One time Lisa had a friend to stay the night and Jane got very drunk and aggressive, Lisa's friend was only 6 and was terrified.

Jane and I were arguing a lot. She would stay in bed for long periods during the day, saying she wasn't well enough to go out so I used to take the kids out quite a lot to get them away from Jane and give them a chance to have fun and enjoy themselves. If Jane was in a good mood I would encourage her to come along. I would often take the kid's friends as well so they could see their friends without coming to the house.

Jane clearly favoured Paul and was much more tactile with him, giving him cuddles and buying him gifts if he did something she believed to be extraordinary. Lisa would have to do a lot more to get her attention. Jane had always insisted that Paul call me Chris rather than Dad, which showed pretty clearly how she felt about me. It is only recently that he started calling me Dad which only now, several years on, is not feeling awkward.

I would dread walking into the house when I came home, not knowing what state she was going to be in. If she was sitting in a particular chair then I knew that she had been drinking. Generally I didn't tell anyone what was going on unless they were involved and saw something, such as the parents of the kid's friends.

It gradually became worse. Jane would become drunk, be verbally abusive and she became very aggressive and would sometimes hold knives, scissors, and beer glasses to my throat. I became very depressed and started to drink whatever was in the house before she did to stop her drinking so much. It didn't work as she bought alcohol that she wouldn't let me drink.

She was paranoid and kept accusing me of having an affair, even someone we passed on the street who I hadn't even noticed or one of her drinking partners. She rifled through things in the house and checked telephone bills to see who I was phoning. Money regularly disappeared and I have no idea how much she was spending on alcohol.

After years of things building up I realised I just wanted to get out, I was very depressed and for the first time thought about suicide. I decided that if I were to commit suicide the kids would get over it but now I realise they wouldn't. I would be driving along to work and see a lorry coming in the opposite direction and think about crossing over to the other side of the road and crashing into the lorry. If Jane and I had argued or she'd done something to annoy or anger me then I'd think about slitting my wrists and writing a message in blood on the walls but was worried the kids would see it rather than Jane. Every time I put them to bed I would tell them that whatever happened I would always love them.

I rejected most of the suicide methods I thought of as I didn't want to affect other people's lives, especially the children. I don't think people had any idea of what I was going through. You can't think clearly and you're not really functioning but are falling to pieces inside. I was on autopilot and strangely able to talk to people and smile for long enough for no-one to ever notice my true state of mind.

I was still able to work but some contract work I was doing at the time was scaled back and I lost work. I was the only one who left and I suspect it was to do with my mental state. I used to go into a meeting room early in the morning and cry. For about six months I spent most of the time thinking about it until my Mum said 'you don't have to stay you know.' After that I felt a lot better because I had choices but things got worse.

I started getting sleep paralysis where your body goes to sleep but your mind doesn't. I could be dreaming I was in danger and couldn't move or wake myself up. On one occasion I managed to wake up and sat up but then I couldn't move for quite a long time. Jane woke up, asked me what I was doing and became abusive. I still couldn't move but eventually after some time I was able to and was shaking. I went to the toilet and ended up on the floor paralysed and shaking. Jane came in and asked me what I was doing. I couldn't answer and she started kicking me. She used the toilet and left me lying on the floor and went back to bed. Eventually I was able to move and went back to bed. I think it may have been a form of epilepsy which is in my family and is brought on by stress.

From when Paul was about 10 he would often break up the arguments and look after Lisa, sleeping on his camp bed in her room. When Paul was about 12 years old Jane came at me with a knife and Paul saw it. He started asking Jane what she was doing and told her that I was the one looking after everyone. She got angry with Paul and went for him with a pair of scissors. Paul and I eventually got them from her and when she went out of the room Paul went and got all sharp implements in the house and hid them. It was about 11pm and Paul went to bed in the same room as Lisa. The next day Paul left the house and went to school, he then went to a friend's house and stayed there for two weeks as he didn't want to come home.

When Lisa was 7, I was on the phone to my brother and I told him 'Jane has a broken glass to my throat right now. There are two outcomes, either I die or she does serious damage and I get the kids'. I was surprised how calm I was and that I was able to give my brother a running commentary about what was happening. I didn't really care if I died and that enabled me to be quite cavalier about the situation. I didn't realise at the time that saying this bought about a change in the balance of power. It was to be another 10 years before she attacked me with a sharp weapon.

Shortly after Paul was away for two weeks I spoke to the kids and asked them what they wanted to do. I told them that I was going to get legal advice and wanted them to live with me. They both said they wanted to be with me and I went to see a few solicitors. I was told that I had a great case but they could not be certain the Courts would give me custody of the kids. There was an 85-90% chance of winning but there were lots of caveats. I had to maintain my income and be at home all the time. My family aren't local and couldn't help out so it wasn't financially possible.

The solicitors admitted that the courts are biased against men. If I moved out and was at work the kids would have to be looked after together by a childminder after school which would exclude them from seeing friends.

I saw two solicitors and offered to double the fees they quoted on a no win no fee basis. Both declined which made me feel my chances were less than they had said. Neither of the solicitors had been involved in a case where a man had won custody of a step child.

One solicitor wrote a letter to Jane saying stop drinking or risk losing your children. My sister suggested I walk out and Jane probably wouldn't cope and so she would hand the kids back to me. I couldn't afford to lose the kids and knew that Jane would use Lisa to get back at me and Paul would be under pressure to cave in and go back to Jane. Jane had in the past complained to Paul several times that she was his Mother and I was not his Father. She would undoubtedly lay the guilt on him so hard and I didn't want to put him through that.

Jane was furious when she got the letter and asked why I hadn't talked to her about it even though I had. She said she wasn't an alcoholic because she didn't drink in the mornings. The letter did have the desired effect and she did stop drinking as much for up to a year. There was a period when she stopped almost completely, just having a few beers and then not drinking for a while. Then she started drinking more heavily, I don't know what caused that. I stayed out of her way when she was drinking and sometimes took the kids as well, even to the supermarket in the early hours of the morning as it was the only warm public place open. We would return when she had either passed out or gone to bed.

Jane was now drinking after she finished work at 2pm and would sometimes be drunk when she collected Lisa from school. She developed health issues due to her alcohol intake and after serious bouts of drinking she would become ill. I spent time taking her to doctors and hospitals. She would be convinced that she was about to die and lie in bed getting us all to do things for her.

She changed jobs and befriended young people who she then went out for drinking sessions with. She also drank at home with loud music which I would ask her to turn down which then started arguments. We used to come into the house without Jane knowing and take what we needed. We disabled the music system so that she couldn't play music loudly in the middle of the night and disturb the neighbours' kids.

After major drinking sessions she had health problems with excessive stomach acid that meant she would be in hospital for a night or two and in bed for a week until she got better and then did it all over again.

It reached the point that Jane had continuous cycles of behaviour; firstly she was very drunk, aggressive & difficult, secondly she became ill through drink and extremely needy and finally nasty and hostile when recovering.

During the first and final phases I was on the receiving end of a stream of abuse such as "you're worthless", "pathetic" and "useless". At the time it all washed over me and I just ignored it. However, these days the cruel taunts tend to come back to haunt me when I am feeling low. They also sap my confidence particularly in front of women I consider approaching.

At one time she could drink up to 40 units of alcohol in a drinking session which could last up to 12 hours. Originally she had drunk cider and had started drinking wine because there was wine in the house. Wine affected her health more so she started drinking lager which affected her less. If she finished the lager and there was wine around she would still drink it, despite knowing it would make her ill the next day.

I know there were occasions when she drank 4 bottles of wine as I saw her drink it. She would hide bottles in the house and garden. I took a photo of the inside of a wardrobe where she had hidden empty bottles and cans and it was completely full. I've still got the photo. She used to pretend she wasn't drinking but if she emptied the bin then I knew there would be bottles hidden in the rubbish.

She gave up her job and was then able to get sickness benefit which she spent on drink, plus child tax credit and money from me which was meant to be for food or house expenses. Over a period of about a year she worked her way through £10,000 and spent it on drink and clothes. At this time she was either ill or permanently drunk. I took voluntary redundancy and was working from home, setting up a business. I was using redundancy money to keep us going so I could be at home and keep an eye on what was going on.

She hated me being at home and this caused more and more friction. I was sleeping on the sofa which was so uncomfortable that I worked until I was exhausted, fell asleep at 5a.m. and got up at 8a.m. I did this for a few years and still don't sleep well - 4 hours is a long night for me. I avoided spending time with her but one time I was so exhausted and she very persistently wanted physical contact. In the end I knew the only way to stop her was to let her and I felt used, abused and worthless.

Lisa was 16 when I was on the computer one time and Jane came up behind me. When I glanced over my shoulder and saw Jane was about to stab me in the back I blocked it with my arm. I had a cut along my arm and the knife went into my back. I turned around and grabbed the knife, cutting my fingers. I was lucky she had made a bad choice of knife which was bendy and not overly sharp. She grabbed the phone and threatened to call the police and tell them I had raped her. She had frequently threatened to do this. The police used to be known to turn up and arrest the male but now they take the whole situation into account. It was 2am and I went and woke Paul up as he was usually able to calm her down. Lisa was woken up from Jane screaming at me. Paul came down and eventually Jane calmed down as he kept telling her to behave and calm down.

I went to see a solicitor about separating and they told me I would have to give Jane half the equity in the house which I couldn't financially achieve. I had always paid the mortgage and I felt stuck. I couldn't just leave the children there and we did wonder if she would accept a much smaller settlement If it was put in front of her in bundles of cash. I encouraged her to leave and wanted to buy her out but she wouldn't go easily. I spoke to my family to see if anyone could lend me money but they couldn't.

I knew Jane was having another affair and eventually I had evidence when she asked me to help her with a problem with her mobile. I saw a message she had sent that made it very clear what was going on. Several months later she told me she was having an affair when she was drunk and a neighbour was also present. I know she'd had a string of one night stands and a few affairs.

It became even more acrimonious between us and that made it easier for me to ignore her if she tried to be amiable and talk about what she wanted financially. Paul was already planning to move out and after he moved out she went to see a solicitor after deciding she wanted to leave. She was advised that we would have to go through mediation for her to get legal aid.

We went twice to mediation and we came to an agreement. I agreed to more than I would have done as Lisa was getting the blunt end of Jane's frustration. At mediation she said she wouldn't drink for a few weeks until she left but she came home and immediately got drunk.

I had agreed at mediation she could leave after Christmas and I got Jane's mother to come down to stay for a few days. I knew if her Mum was there she wouldn't make any trouble. After Christmas I had to ask her to pack her bags which she didn't want to do and then drove her and her mother back home.

At Paul's wedding Jane made a big effort to ingratiate herself with my family. She clearly wanted to get back together. She invited me back to her room and kept asking me to dance. I refused and she went after another man in an attempt to make me jealous. She said it was the worst wedding she'd ever been to. Paul was really upset and didn't want to have anything to do with her for a few months and rarely sees her now.

Lisa sees Jane every 2-3 months and is always stressed when she sees her Mum as she worries that she will have been drinking. After seeing Lisa, Jane pesters her after a couple of weeks to see her again. She often calls off meetings at the last minute which upsets Lisa.

What kept me going? After my Mum said I didn't have to stay, that helped. I took each day at a time and didn't look ahead. I still do that and can't plan things ahead. The only goal I have is to enjoy the day and I don't have any long term goals. I find myself doing simple unproductive things that will occupy my mind enough to stop myself thinking about the things I don't want to think about. When I was with Jane I was always finding that she would be the main reason why I had trouble completing long jobs or keeping commitments. Now I have difficulty starting anything that will take more than a few minutes and will find myself avoiding it, even things I enjoy and want to do. I also hate having my life mapped out in front of me. I feel lost and have no idea of where I want to be and consequently no idea how to get there.

What have I learnt about myself? I'm too tolerant. I don't think there is that much I could have done, apart from leave. That would have meant that the children were left with a drunk.

Going forward I know I've got a problem with trust. I'm making judgements of people all the time. Many people I meet of my age are either thinking of leaving a relationship or have just split up. It's sad but there seems to be a growing trend to split up as the children start to leave home.

Lisa is less trusting of women and for a time found it difficult to make friends, but thankfully this is now improving. Paul is living nearby and married.

I feel resigned to not being with someone and sometimes am comfortable with that but I hope it doesn't turn out like that. I don't know what my position will be when Lisa moves out and I'm on my own. I'll be very lonely although I've always been quite happy being alone. I've never been someone who will sleep with anyone they meet. I need to know someone and be comfortable with them first. If I did get close to someone I would find it difficult to move away from them. My fear is making a bad choice and I don't want to repeat the traumatic experience again.

Despite all the misery with Jane, it took me a long time for me to get to the point when I wanted to leave. I always wanted things to get better and didn't want to confront the situation. If I hook up with someone who is bad for me I may have difficulty leaving them or ending the relationship. I have lost a lot of friends since knowing Jane as she didn't like me spending time with them.

At the time the things that Jane did to Lisa affected me more than what she did to me. The things that affected me most were when Jane sulked, didn't talk to me, didn't want to be tactile unless she wanted sex and the fact that she didn't really want to be with me was really upsetting. I believe that throughout the relationship she wanted to be with Paul's Dad rather than me. This didn't prevent me attempting to locate Paul's Dad when Paul expressed the desire to meet him. When we eventually found him Jane made a point of being there and much to my amusement she was hugely disappointed that he wasn't what she expected.

The only time she was really nice to me was when I had the redundancy money. She was a compulsive liar and would lie even when we knew something wasn't true and I don't know whether this was also caused by the drink. I'd find myself constantly wondering what she was really thinking or doing. I can't remember a lot of what happened with Jane, I think it's a defence mechanism so I won't go back to thinking about how bad things were.

I think a lot of people who are in a similar situation, particularly men, would just leave. If there were no kids I think they should try and get the drinker to get help first and if that didn't work then I would advise they leave. Jane didn't admit she had a problem until later on. She went to a meeting for alcoholics once and ended up in the pub!

Working things out if you can is good; we all have things we could improve. You have to think about what you each want and whether there is anything you can do to improve the situation.

I am now comfortable about myself and although I was never good at approaching women, I've got better. I used to comfort eat and I've lost a lot of weight, about 6 stone. I am now a lot fitter, more relaxed and feel more positive than the previous 20 years.

Chapter 13: Caroline

For many years I didn't go out much as I had 2 children from my first marriage. I occasionally went to meet a good friend at the local pub and one day he introduced me to Peter. We got on really well and after meeting again in the pub for a drink he asked me out to dinner a few weeks later. We only went out twice before he went abroad for a few weeks holiday. He wrote to me and we spoke on the phone several times whilst he was away. Despite the distance it was a whirlwind romance. He bought me gifts before leaving and arranged to have flowers delivered on several occasions while he was away.

When he returned to the UK a couple of weeks later and asked me to marry him I accepted. I was thrilled as I really believed that I knew enough about him to feel that we would grow old together. A couple of weeks later he moved in with me and the children. At first he got on really well with my children and made an effort to talk to them, wanted us all to eat together in the evenings, and talked about subjects that interested them. I remember when we first met he said that he had never been in a house that had so much laughter.

He had 2 children from a previous marriage and they seemed pleased that Peter had met someone after being alone for a long time. I got on well with them and it all seemed pretty perfect. I was incredibly happy, happier than I'd ever been before.

I knew that he usually went to the pub for 2 to 3 hours on a Friday night and occasionally I would meet him there. I didn't have a problem with him going out on a Friday night as he explained that he had met most of his friends at the pub and that it was a tradition to meet on a Friday. He went to an exercise class on a Saturday morning which was a long drive away and he would often not come home until mid-afternoon as the traffic had been bad. It took me a while to realise that he was going to the pub afterwards on the way home. Once I realised, I questioned him and he said it was his way of winding down after a stressful week at work. On Sunday's early afternoon he would go out for a variety of reasons and I didn't realise that he always ended up at the pub. Sometimes he said he needed peace and quiet to do some work and told me where he was going, I just didn't realise it was so regular.

About 6 months after he moved in I first realised he sometimes stopped off at the pub on the way home for a 'quick one'. He often called to say that a meeting had gone on late or the trains were delayed. I used to feel sorry for him as he left home early and got back late. He smoked and then had a mint on the way home in the car which disguised the smell of beer.

We married 8 months after we started living together and after about 2 months I noticed a marked change in his behaviour. I asked him what the problem was as he was at the pub all the time. I asked him if he was unhappy or whether I had done anything wrong. A month later he had a couple of weeks off and was at the pub on most days. He started to become withdrawn, sulky and moody. This continued and was particularly noticeable on a Sunday if he didn't go the pub.

He came up with all kinds of 'reasons' for drinking: work was stressful, living with 2 teenagers that aren't his own, our living conditions were making him feel claustrophobic and he needed some time on his own as he had been on his own for many years before we married.

He promised he wouldn't go to the pub every day once we moved into our new house and said it would be good for him to live further away from the local pub that he always went to. He told me that the reason he had gone away when we first met was because he needed time away to help him get out of the habit of drinking 6 pints each night on the way home from work.

What really upset me was that he drank and drove on a regular basis yet he was convinced that drinking made no difference to his driving. I talked to him and when things didn't change, wrote to him about drinking and driving and the possible consequences to him and the family but it didn't change, despite his promises to cut down.

After we moved to a new area I initially thought he was working late and then found out he was making a detour and driving an additional 30 minutes to drink at his old local pub. He then started to drink at pubs local to where we were living. I realised this was the case when we walked into one and the barman gave him his 'usual' and pulled him a pint before he asked for it!

On Saturdays he still made a detour to go to the old pub. If he had a day off, felt stressed or fancied a pint then he always went to the old pub in the afternoon for a few hours. He said it was his way of relaxing. I did ask him why he needed to go and why he wasn't interested in sitting in the garden for a glass of wine with me. He said 'It wasn't the same' and that he preferred to go to the pub but couldn't explain why.

He took 2 days off and the day before my birthday went shopping for my presents and then went to the pub in the afternoon. On my birthday my son was ill and we couldn't go out for lunch as planned so he went to the pub at 12.30pm and returned at 7.30pm. On my birthday he didn't have dinner with me or give me my presents for a few days. Initially I felt bad that buying presents caused him so much stress but later realised that buying me a present for Christmas or my birthday gave him the excuse to drink heavily on a couple of occasions for each event.

A couple of months later we were due to meet friends locally for a drink. They called me as they saw Peter in the old pub and thought we were meeting there. Peter came home immediately and I confronted him as to why he was unable to wait 15 minutes for a beer. This was the first time I got very upset. He was quiet and said he would go to the pub less often, stop smoking, start exercising, lose weight, become healthier, etc. He had said this on many other occasions and I had spent some time talking to him, offering support and ideas as to what he could do. He made no changes and usually after he made promises he would drink and smoke more.

On a few occasions I arranged to meet him for a drink on a Friday evening at 6.00pm and when he arrived at the train station I realised he had already had a drink. He cannot just drink 1 pint and became agitated if I wanted to leave the pub after one drink if we were both driving.

A year after we were married I went away with the children and my family for the weekend to celebrate my parent's golden wedding anniversary. Peter had been invited but didn't want to go. I heard later that he had gone to the pub both Friday evening and Saturday afternoon. On Saturday evening friends tried to drive him home from the pub but he refused. They followed him to a take away restaurant where he parked in the middle of the car park and apparently found it difficult to stand upright when placing an order. They again offered to drive him home and he refused. Sunday afternoon he also went to the pub and when we returned early evening he fell asleep at the dinner table due to the amount he had drunk.

The following few months I knew he was going to the pub on a daily basis and I started to be able to tell when he'd had a lot to drink as he repeated the same conversations 10 minutes later, swayed slightly and didn't remember conversations the next day. I began to become a bit obsessed with how much he was drinking and fearful that he wouldn't come home at night if he had an accident.

I wrote Peter emails about his drinking and driving as talking to him had no effect. His daughter was involved in a car accident having spent Saturday afternoon in the pub with him. She was arrested after being breathalysed but later just managed to pass the blood test while in police custody. He was shocked and on the way to the police station said it was his fault and that he shouldn't have been drinking so much as he had also been driving. I thought that would help motivate him to stop drinking and driving but it didn't.

I felt betrayed and confused as I didn't feel I knew who he really was. He had originally been so loving, caring, humorous and protective but now seemed withdrawn, emotionally distant, moody and full of anger. He did eventually tell me that he'd been drinking heavily for the last 40 years and had started when he found it easier to socialise. I now realise that the reason his hands shook in the mornings was due to alcohol withdrawal, I was so naive.

I called his daughters a month later and said I was very concerned about him as he had been to the doctors and been told he was overweight, had high cholesterol and had early signs of diabetes. His daughter told me that he had been told this a few times over the years and he didn't make any changes. She said he was very obstinate and ignored them when they had told him that he needed to exercise and cut down on beer.

If we went out I usually drove so that I didn't have to worry about him drinking and driving. We had a few arguments when he insisted on driving on one occasion and I wouldn't get into the car unless he let me drive. He believed he could have 4 pints of beer, 5 glasses of wine and still be alright to drive.

I organised the family finances and realised that he was spending about £600 a month and I had asked him what he was spending so much money on. He said there must be some mistake and someone else must have taken his debit card or bank details. A few weeks later I asked him if he had checked with the Bank and he confirmed they were his withdrawals and claimed that it wasn't all spent at the pub.

I started drinking more as it made me less angry when he didn't come home and made me less fearful that he was going to crash the car/injure someone/injure himself/have a heart attack, etc. After a few months I realised what I was doing and returned to my usual habit of drinking only at the weekend.

I started to withdraw from him to protect myself from being hurt, upset and angry. I told him that I was no longer going to worry about him drinking and driving or his health. He seemed pleased with this and said I was becoming a nag and several times told me that I reminded him of his mother. This worried me as he'd told me that his Mother had made him really angry and eventually his Father told him to leave home as he'd tried to hit his Mother.

His ideal weekend was to lie in bed in the morning watching cookery programmes, get up, sometimes potter around in the garden for a while, then go to the pub, come back late afternoon, fall asleep in front of the TV, eat and go to bed. I told him he was free to do as he wanted and spend all weekend at the pub if that was what he wanted. I wasn't going to wait around for him to come home, I was going to get on with my life and do the things I wanted to do at the weekend.

He continued to drink at the pub and at home over Christmas and said he was going to cut down in the New Year. In January I thought he wasn't drinking during the week but realised he was stopping off at a pub in London or on the way back from work. He was regularly lying to me about where he was and friends said they always saw his car in the old pub car park when they drove past.

Mid-January I spoke to a few people on the phone at Al - anon as I wasn't sure if I was being unreasonable about his drinking habits. I gave details of his behaviour and mood swings and their opinion was that he was a "top-up alcoholic". He was never so drunk that he completely fell over or was physically ill. I couldn't tell what mood he would come home in, he could be in a really good mood and it would change suddenly, he would become angry with something on TV or something that had happened that day such as someone talking loudly on their mobile on the train! At the weekend he would sleep as long as possible, have little energy and feel very down. He would get sugar cravings and eat 5 snack bars one after the other or drink a bottle of Lucozade with sugary snacks.

I knew he was going to the pub every day as I could smell it on his breath. I went to an Al-Anon meeting without his knowledge. They advised me not to tell him to ensure he didn't dissuade me from going. Listening to other peoples experiences at the meeting I realised that alcoholism is a very long term illness. I met people whose partners had stopped drinking for some years and then started again. Others had partners who would not stop and were in and out of hospital. Some had taken years to leave their partners and were still attending meetings. It was a wake-up call and I realised that I didn't want to be going to meetings in years to come with the rollercoaster of hope and despair.

I started sleeping in the spare room, making the excuse of work commitments and having to get up early, a bad cold, his snoring etc. I had got to the point where I was finding it difficult to be close to him as I had lost respect for him. One Saturday evening after he'd been to the pub and fallen asleep on the sofa watching TV he became angry and said he was fed up with me being distant, polite but not close to him and walked out of the room, refusing to talk. He went to bed and later said he hadn't meant that he'd had enough of us but had enough of situation. I said I also had had enough and couldn't take any more. I told him that I'd been to the Al – anon meeting and he was shocked.

We were both in tears and he said he'd do whatever it took to save the marriage. He said he would stop drinking and smoking if I would give him one last chance and I agreed. I suggested he may be an alcoholic and he was shocked. He agreed that he would get some help and I said he needed to arrange that himself.

I had been having migraines every 2 weeks during the last few months due to the stress at home. On this occasion I was still vomiting well into the evening and this time he looked after me rather than going to the pub. The day after, we talked and he admitted he had been very selfish and not aware of the effect his behaviour had been having on me. He did not know why he was so moody and down most of the time. He said he couldn't remember when he had been really happy and there wasn't much joy in his life. I'm not sure whether he realised what he was saying when we had only been together for just over 2 years and he certainly seemed very happy about getting married.

He said he hadn't understood what getting married really meant, that it was a partnership and that you had to think about the other person and their needs. He said he had thought it was an arrangement of convenience!

He went to see a Therapist I had recommended to him and then went on to the pub. I came back home to find him elated and full of hope. He seemed more positive and optimistic for the next few days and we were more relaxed together and I was hopeful that things would change.

A few days later he said that if he was still 'a moody person' in a year then it was probably best if we went our separate ways. Unfortunately the following weekend he went back to the usual pattern of going to the pub and sleeping in front of the TV. He was in a bad mood all weekend and didn't want to talk. He didn't realise that I knew he was drinking and smoking again, after seeing tobacco in the pocket of a jacket I took to the dry cleaners. He was chewing gum on a regular basis and also eating a lot of mints.

The following weekend was a friend's party and he said he wasn't going to drink much and would drive. I couldn't help watching how much he drank - he had at least 5 pints that I saw at the party and went outside regularly for a cigarette. He decided he wanted to leave and that he would drive home. I had enjoyed the evening dancing and hadn't worried about what he was doing or how much he was drinking but knew it must be a lot and on a regular basis to be able to have 5 pints and for it not to show. He had driven, was talking coherently and not swaying.

He went for another session with the Therapist and said his session had gone well. Later he mentioned he'd gone onto the pub afterwards and seen mutual friends. He was repeating himself in the conversation and it was clear he must have had a lot to drink. My initial hopes started to fade and I had a huge sense of disappointment and felt betrayed after all his promises.

A few days later he asked to talk to me and I asked him why he had been going to the pub so much. He said he didn't know, was sorry etc. I told him that I'd had enough and the marriage was over. He said that he knew that he'd completely f....... things up and that it was his fault the marriage was over. He said he couldn't believe that he'd been so stupid and didn't understand why he hadn't listened to me. He also said this might be the huge 'kick up the arse' that he needed to make him change.

I moved into the guest room permanently and we agreed to keep things as civil as possible because of the children. He told me some weeks later that I didn't make things clear to him and hadn't told him that the marriage was over if he didn't stop drinking. He said that he didn't want a separation or divorce and wanted another chance. Peter became very angry once he realised that I was serious and wasn't going to give him yet another chance. He repeatedly told me that I'd been scheming and deceitful as I had gone to the Al – anon meeting without his knowledge! I had talked, pleaded, shouted, cried and written to him about his drinking. Now he said he couldn't remember any of that and that I should have screamed and shaken him to get him to listen. I realise that this was another occasion when I was being blamed for my behaviour rather than him taking responsibility for his own behaviour.

Once I had made my mind up it was very clear to me that I had to follow it through. I knew how many times he had made promises and then done the opposite and I didn't want to be like the other people I'd met at Al – anon who had stayed with their partners who were going in and out of hospital with alcohol related illnesses. I felt broken-hearted as I had loved him more than any other man. Whether he really was that man I'd fallen in love with was another question. I also felt a huge sense of failure as it was my second marriage and I would never have got married if I'd thought it was going to end in divorce. We had a beautiful house and garden but it wasn't enough for him. I know that if he had to choose between the pub and me it would be the pub that he'd choose.

We lived together for another 8 months and it was hell. Initially Peter was polite but after a few weeks he started to drink more and I didn't know if he was going to come home humming very loudly in an apparently good mood or talking to himself, swearing at me and the children. We kept out of his way as much as possible as he went through all the possible tactics to get me to respond and give him attention. One time he was very nice and suddenly cooked us all dinner, then he started ignoring me and then apologised saying he was so upset and angry that he couldn't trust himself to talk or look at me. I think he was hoping that I would feel guilty or sorry for him and change my mind.

We put the house on the market and I started putting everything in writing to make sure there was a record as his memory seemed to be getting worse and he repeatedly denied conversations we'd had. I really wanted to move out but needed to keep the house looking presentable for viewings. Peter's behaviour became increasingly erratic.

On one occasion after drinking all afternoon and evening in the pub he returned home drunk. We were watching a film and had the sound turned up loud but did not realise that he went straight to bed. About 15 minutes later we heard 2 bangs and Peter burst into the room swearing and shouting at us. He continued to shout and was extremely angry. I told him that we hadn't realised he'd gone to bed and he just needed to ask us to turn the TV down, that there was no need to get angry or shout. We turned the sound down immediately and he continued to complain angrily. He left the room and went back upstairs, still swearing and slamming doors.

My son decided he wanted to go up to his bedroom but returned shortly after as he said Peter was still shouting and swearing. We all stayed downstairs for another 15 minutes and then the boys decided they wanted to go to bed. I went up with them to make sure there were no further problems and that Peter was now quiet and asleep.

In the past Peter had been loud and occasionally angry but this was quite frightening as I could tell he had been drinking and there was a great deal of anger due to our current situation. He never physically hurt me but did shout and threaten me by coming up close to my face and saying I had better agree to something or else. He also said that he could make a phone call to people he knew that could be hired and I would never know when that might happen. I was scared of him and kept out of his way as much as possible. I became extremely nervous and constantly woke up in the night if I heard any sounds. The bedroom didn't have a lock on the door and I started to sleep with a baseball bat under my bed which was ridiculous but made me feel safer. I lost a great deal of weight and the lack of sleep affected my work but I was advised not to leave the house until it was sold.

He deliberately did things to get my attention and engage me in conversation in order that he could shout and argue but I ignored it. There was no point in having conversations with him as afterwards he either refuted it or refused to accept the conversation had taken place.

After 8 months on the market the house sold and I moved out quickly after we exchanged without Peter knowing I was going as I knew he would make things very difficult. He had started packing a month earlier, deliberately removing some of my books and cd's but I had ignored this as it would only have resulted in an argument. We waited until he went to work and literally packed and moved out in a day. I subsequently heard that he told people at the pub that I had taken everything, even his children! I also heard that I was having an affair, that I was the one with a drink problem and drinking a bottle of whisky a day! I didn't take anything that hadn't been owned by me prior to the marriage or that we had agreed, I didn't want anything of his.

He refused to attend mediation, saying I could make all the appointments I wanted but he wouldn't turn up. I was advised by a Mediator experienced in working with alcoholics that my best option was to go to Court. Unfortunately it was a fiasco, the reason for the divorce was completely ignored and due to him not having a pension he was awarded half the assets despite me having 2 children. This resulted in me losing a great deal of money that I'd had before we were married. I was angry at first and then decided that if that was what I'd had to pay to get out of the marriage then it was worth it!

I have learnt that I'm far stronger than I realised and that whilst I really wanted to have a partner to grow old with, I am far happier on my own. It's been two years since the relationship ended and I still have no interest in having another relationship. At this time I cannot imagine ever spending the night with someone or getting close. I have a lot of good friends that I see regularly and some of them are men as I like men and still enjoy their company.

The last couple of years I have concentrated on my children and creating a stable home for us. I am really focused on what I want to achieve in the next five years and part of that is wisely investing the remaining money I have so that I can reach financial stability again.

If I met anyone in a similar situation I would encourage them to talk about it and take a step back to look at what was happening. When you're in a situation like that you start to lose a sense of reality and question yourself as you feel you must have done something to cause or contribute to it. I am very grateful to a good friend of mine who asked the question "Do you think he might be an alcoholic?"

Initially I was dismissive and came up with all of his "reasons" for drinking. It was only after reflecting on events and behaviours that I started to look at the situation more objectively. After I'd left I did have some help through talking to a Therapist and it helped me accept what has happened and move forward.

I would suggest people look at what they were like before the relationship and how they are now. If you feel that you've changed negatively and that it's a direct result of living with an alcoholic then you have choices as to what you do. There are many ways of deciding how to cope with living with an alcoholic. You can leave things as they are and not change anything. You can stay and focus on your own life which is likely to result in having to put some mental and physical distance between you and your partner. Or you can end the relationship and leave.

I have been so lucky to have strong support from my parents and friends and that's been really important. Al – anon are really supportive and a good way of getting a reality check. Personally I didn't go for more sessions as I felt I could move on by myself. I didn't want to be constantly going over the past and whilst it's important to learn from the past I now want to focus on the future.

Chapter 14: Diane

We first met Christmas 1976 at a night club, I was just 15 and had recently split up from my first boyfriend. I was living at home and he was living with his mother. He was two years older than me and was a very caring, loving person who made me laugh. My dad was very strict and said very little. There was nothing dreadful about my upbringing but there wasn't much love so having love and affection from Charles was wonderful. I was a confident person, despite not doing that well at school and I started studying to be a secretary. I excelled and started working in the holidays as a temporary secretary. I left school at 17 and Charles was working as a plumber. I went to work in London and I always seemed to earn more than him which never bothered me. We used to go for a drink after work and it was the one time in my life that I drank quite a lot but I didn't really enjoy it. Charles used to come up to London to meet me and colleagues after work.

I became pregnant when I was 18 and my parents never knew. I had an abortion as they wouldn't have thought it was the right thing to do and Charles felt the same. Charles came from a single parent family and had never known his Dad. There were a lot of other family around although his Mum had gone away to have him.

When I was 19 we decided to buy a place together but as we didn't have a large deposit I asked my Dad to help but he refused because he didn't want us to live together and in his opinion we were too young to get married. We saved the money and went ahead. Dad disowned me and didn't talk to me for 3 years. If I went home to see them he would behave as though I wasn't there. Dad would go to the pub every night and at the weekend. He wasn't an alcoholic but drink was an issue. He worked long hours as well so we didn't see much of him. I think he was disappointed with me and that made me determined to do well and get my own place. He did hit me once and I rushed off to see Charles.

Charles started drinking and now I look back I can see a few things. I wasn't aware of Charles's mother drinking but she was diabetic and smoked heavily. She was told she needed to give up smoking or she would lose a leg. She didn't stop and ended up having her leg removed in a London hospital. I went to see her regularly on my way home which seemed to bother Charles as he felt he should be going. I think he saw it as a failing and as I earned more than him he saw that as a failing as well. Charles was self-employed and I did his books for him and organised all the household money.

When I was 22 we moved home. Charles entered a competition and won a van. We decided that when we sold his old one then we would get married and he could have a course to learn to fly which was a passion of his.

When I look back we had some drink fuelled arguments and were close to splitting up. We were a Jekyll and Hyde couple. We went out and everyone thought we were fine. We went on holiday and met a group of people, some of whom were heavy drinkers. One night I went to bed and said he could go out drinking. As we had one key I had asked him to lock me in before going out. The next morning he hadn't come home and I couldn't get out. I waited until I could see someone on another balcony and asked them for help. From the balcony I could see him coming back from the beach. They'd had so much to drink and I was angry with the person who got him drunk rather than him for drinking. There were other incidents and many times when he drank which caused us to argue. I did think about finishing with him but was afraid of how he would react.

Before the wedding Charles's mother had to have her other leg amputated. She had to move as she couldn't live where she was and went into warden assisted housing. She came out of hospital and we had arranged everything for her so that it was comfortable. I was always the driving force behind everything and took that for granted. In our relationship we never had a joint bank account.

Before we got married I realised that I couldn't remember if I was going to promise to obey. I asked the vicar and he said I had wanted to and said it was too late to change. I don't remember saying it and it became something that Charles would bring up in our arguments. He would tell me "You will obey" and this would make me rebel as I didn't want to feel I couldn't be my own person.

In the first year of marriage when we had been together for 7 years, there was a lot of drinking. On our 1st wedding anniversary we had a huge argument; Charles had been drinking, stormed out and drove off. He was stopped and banned from driving which he took badly. I had to take him to see his Mum if he wanted to see her. His Mum went on the first holiday she'd had since the amputations and she died in her sleep when she was only 57 and we had to go and identify her. I organised all the funeral and Charles started drinking particularly heavily.

Charles was self-employed but worked with a group of people who supported him and carried him through a few difficult years. He got a sizeable inheritance from his mother despite his concern that money would be a problem. I felt he should do what he wanted with the money as I earned more than him and was still working in London. He put about £10,000 into doing up the house, leaving about £50,000. With a couple of friends he bought a share in an aircraft as his dream was to be a commercial pilot. He didn't pass his class 1 medical to allow him to fly at night as he was colour blind which affected him badly and he started drinking even more. I was always making excuses for his drinking such as 'its because of his mother', 'not being able to fly', etc.

When the house refurbishment was finished I was 27 years old and couldn't see us having children at that point. Charles would have liked children earlier but I felt we needed more space and we started to look for somewhere to move. We argued a lot and I remember having a huge argument when we were house hunting, just before we found the house we wanted to buy. It was our dream house and we moved in when I was 29. Charles loved the house and said the only way he would move out was when he was in a wooden box.

After Charles's drink ban was over he sold his share in the plane and became a bus and coach driver. I remember him coming home once quite drunk. He was arrested and accused of exposing himself on a train. He claimed he had been drunk and the charge was dropped, I don't know what really happened.

I used to go horse riding and one day when I came back home he couldn't talk and could hardly breathe. I followed the ambulance to hospital where they diagnosed pleurisy, pneumonia and a collapsed lung. He was ill for a long time and I think it was from that point on that the drinking started to get worse. He had always been reasonably fit but he was putting on weight and drinking a lot and I didn't realise the increase in weight was due to drinking.

I was still working in London and spent time travelling to work and horse riding. I had ridden for many years and had always wanted my own horses. I bought my own horse who I didn't know was in foal. She produced a beautiful colt and they kept me sane. I stopped working in London when I was 34 as I found commuting so hard and I thought if we were going to have children I couldn't work in London. I had also started to lose confidence and faith in my achievements. I think this was because I felt I wasn't dealing well with what was happening at home. I found it stressful going through the interview process due to lack of confidence but got a good job fairly locally.

I had a bad car accident on my way to an event and amazingly I wasn't badly hurt and was able to get out of the car although the car was a right-off. I was taken by ambulance to hospital and the people I was going to meet collected me from hospital. I called Charles to let him know that I was alright and would see him the next day. The accident changed my attitude to life; I used to ask myself if things mattered as I had survived. I never went into shock after the accident. I just kept going and felt I had to carry on. That's the way I've always been - I'm a survivor.

I left my job six months later and got a job very close to home. I still didn't acknowledge that drink was Charles's problem. I blamed it on other things but as time went on he put on more weight. I did realise that I wasn't sure if I wanted to be with him anymore but wasn't sure how he would react if I left him. We had lots of arguments as we started getting into debt and the house wasn't being refurbished as planned. I would come home and find things weren't being done properly and I don't know whether it was because he was drinking. I felt that if I didn't organise it then it wouldn't be right. It was only if we had a big argument that he would then do any work around the house. He went through phases where he didn't want to do work he was trained in and would think about what else he could do.

We had a school reunion after 25 years of leaving school. I met a man that I'd been seeing just before my husband and it was like fireworks. I asked him not to call me as I knew what might happen. He was unhappily married and I could imagine being with him. We did meet a few months later with friends. I was confused as I had been thinking about having a child with Charles but couldn't stop seeing John. I fell pregnant and spent the whole pregnancy wondering whose baby it was which was terrible. John and I agreed to stop seeing each other and luckily when Andrew was born he was the spitting image of Charles. A year before getting pregnant I did tell Charles I wasn't sure if I wanted to be with him anymore. He went off and got really drunk and I left a message begging him to come home. After this I thought we should stay together and make a go of things.

I was very small when I was pregnant. The birth was a bit traumatic and I went into shock afterwards as it had happened very fast at the end. I didn't hold Andrew initially and he was born just before Christmas so we spent time at home together. Now I look back at photos I can see Charles was drunk in all the photos.

I was on maternity leave for 5 months and during that time we fell apart and I found out he owed a lot of money and had four years of books to sort out. I spent most of my maternity leave helping him and felt cheated of my time with Andrew.

New neighbours moved in and the grandmother looked after Andrew for me. I established some contact with John again who had split up from his wife and was seeing other women. I realised that John also drank a lot and as he had told me some of the things that had happened in his marriage I knew he had tried to control his wife. I had alarm bells going and I thought I wouldn't be able to cope with him as he was disruptive.

I wasn't sure how I felt about Charles despite having Andrew. I went back to work and I started to find empty bottles everywhere in the house but I still wouldn't accept it was alcoholism. He went to the doctor for depression and the doctor suggested he went to AA (Alcoholics Anonymous). He went onto medication for his depression and went a couple of times to AA meetings. They told me about Al-Anon but I didn't see that I had a problem and couldn't see why I needed to go. A friend of mine also suggested Al-Anon to me and when Andrew was about 2 years old I finally realised Charles had a serious problem.

I had been calling Charles's work to say he was unwell when he was drunk. One time I called work for him and they said unless he came into work he wouldn't have a job. So I told them he was drunk and that was why he couldn't come in. He lost his job and that was my low point and I called Al-Anon. The first meeting I went to was a revelation because all the stories were so similar. I realised that I needed to share my experience without resulting in an argument which is what happened at home.

I let go of trying to control his drinking by pouring any drink away and he started to get worse. As long as it was safe to do so then I left the drink where I found it. Even Andrew was finding bottles and used to toddle over and bring them to Charles. I would worry about leaving Andrew in Charles's care but needed to go to Al-Anon. Hearing shared stories of other people was heart wrenching, I had compassion for other alcoholics but struggled to have compassion for Charles. I used to say the serenity prayer over and over in my head. Charles used me going to Al-Anon as an excuse to drink more. He still knew how to push my buttons and then used that as an excuse to drink.

Charles went through about ten jobs in the 2 years I'd been going to Al-Anon. In Al-Anon there were people whose partners were in recovery and I hoped we'd be able to work it out. He was a binge drinker and could avoid drinking heavily for a couple of months and then drink to excess and be completely out of it.

After I went to Al-Anon I stopped watching and recording how much he drank as I learned to let go. I was still in charge of the finances and gave him some money which he resented but it was the only way I could make sure we didn't get into debt. If he wanted money for drink then he would do private jobs for cash. One time he'd been drinking with a friend who called me to say Charles was in a bad state and he wanted me to come and get him. I couldn't leave Andrew and Al-Anon had taught me I had to let go as long as Andrew and I were safe and Charles wasn't in any physical danger. He eventually came back paralytic, knocked on the door and hid behind the bush.

On my 40th birthday I arranged a dinner at a restaurant. Charles was drunk as he had been on a binge a few days before. I was really upset as he hadn't come out of it in time for my birthday. The morning of my birthday he came in and wanted to have sex but I didn't want to and felt it would be rape so I ran out of the house. I told Charles I wanted a divorce and he was really upset. That evening we went to the restaurant and they didn't have a record of the reservation. It was rearranged for another venue but was an awful evening. Charles was in tears and told people I wanted a divorce and that he loved Andrew and me so much.

I asked him to sleep in the caravan as I didn't want to share a bedroom with him. He begged me not to divorce him and I hoped that this was his 'rock bottom' and that he would come up from this. He'd had lots of rock bottoms in the two years since I'd been going to Al-Anon. I grew away from him and found it hard to have a relationship with him. I knew that he was going to see escort girls and I didn't mind as I didn't have sex with him much and found it painful since giving birth to Andrew. I think the pain was because I didn't want a physical relationship and couldn't give him the love he so needed. In the past our relationship in bed had been good and in many ways kept the relationship going. Without this I wondered what was left. I first realised he was seeing escort girls when I noticed cheques for £350 and I called him and asked what they were for and told him he didn't have money for paying escort girls.

Things started disappearing from the house. He had a job where he got them to pay him £2,000 up front. They recognised he had a drinking problem, changed their minds and asked for the money back but he had already spent the money. When he was on a binge he could get through £1,000 easily and a binge could last up to two weeks. I had to get a loan from my father to pay them back. I remember answering the phone to a woman who said Charles owed her money for computer parts. We didn't have a computer and I knew that it was for an escort girl. I told her he didn't have money and that he had done it before, that he was a drunk and to be careful in the future.

I told Charles that he should pay his debts and I didn't care if he saw escort girls, my only concern was that I didn't catch anything as I slept with him occasionally. I think I didn't mind because I felt I should be sleeping with him more.

I changed jobs as I couldn't leave Andrew with Charles in the evening. One weekend I went away for an Al-Anon Convention and friends had Andrew. When I came back Charles was at friends and they said he was very drunk and they brought him home.

We were going caravanning with friends and Andrew was in the car ready to go. Charles and I had an argument and he hit me. I called the police and they stayed with Charles while I went away with Andrew. The next day he arrived drunk, he often drank and drove. He was in a state and friends kept him away from Andrew and me. That night he was meant to go but he appeared and was banging on the caravan door, we kept quiet and eventually he went away. I told him he had to move out and he made a big effort and I thought he had turned a corner. I thought I should give him back his independence and gave him his bank cards back. I took Andrew to see a friend for a week and when I came back Charles collected us from the airport. He didn't seem too bad but then he started drinking again and I knew he could go downhill quickly and get us into debt again.

I saw a solicitor, the police and people at the Domestic Violence and Abuse Bureau. I got a Court Injunction to get Charles out of the house because of the potential danger to Andrew and me. If I called the police when Charles was being abusive, he could sober up really quickly and I started to wonder if people would think I was the irrational one. If I was dressed up to go out somewhere Charles would tell me I looked like a slut.

When Charles left I knew he was homeless and it was really hard. My Aunt called me and said she wanted to offer him a home which I was glad about but I did warn her about his drinking and money problems. I took Andrew over to see him and he moved out to somewhere more local to us. He lasted a few months before starting to drink again and lost his job. I was struggling to cope with everything and felt I wasn't really moving on.

Charles used to see Andrew regularly and have him for overnight contact. I was quite uncomfortable about this but knew that Charles really loved Andrew and felt that if he was sober when he picked Andrew up then everything would be alright. In the summer Charles took Andrew away for two weeks. I spoke to Andrew daily and they were having a great time until a few days before they were due to return. I spoke to Charles and realised that he had been drinking. Charles did not return Andrew and the police were involved in Andrews' safe return. I had to fill out a 'missing persons' report for both Charles and Andrew. I felt Andrew was safe but I was also fearful that I might have got this wrong. The Serenity Prayer and my Al-Anon friends were my saviour.

Following this there were various contact orders for Andrew and arrangements were made for Charles to see Andrew at a contact centre every week. I could sometimes tell that Charles had been drinking but I didn't stop him seeing him. Charles wanted more contact and we went to Court a few times to sort out contact issues and the divorce. The judges didn't seem to understand that Charles would drink and drive whilst looking after Andrew. It was agreed that we would pick up and drop off at the police station, Charles often turned up drunk but I let him see Andrew.
Charles met a nice girl friend called Louise who he moved in with. The Court ruled that Andrew could stay with them on the understanding that Charles wouldn't drink. I tried to be open minded and what I had learnt at the A Anon helped. I said the serenity prayer a lot. I went to AA open meetings where you listen but don't share. It made me realise that I had taken on so much of Charles's rubbish it was almost as though it had happened to me. It enabled me to understand how he was thinking and why he did what he did.

The final Court hearing was June 2004. The Court ruled that I had to move out of the house which I was really angry about as I had paid for so much and got him out of his debts. My Dad was in hospital on the Court day and Mum went into hospital the next day after a heart attack. I spent the following week going to the hospital and Dad had to go into a home. I was due to move out of the house, it was very stressful and I felt completely out of control. People came to help me, including friends from Al-Anon. I found it difficult to throw things out and let things go, I had too much but wasn't ready to throw things away. It was very traumatic. Dad was unhappy in the home and I told him I'd look at other homes when I got back from a week away with Andrew. I got back and Dad died three days later after a chest infection. My decree nisi came through that day, it was a hard time as Mum wasn't well either.

Charles went on holiday with his girlfriend and he drank too much and Louise didn't know what to do with him. Louise took Charles to his aunt and they arranged for him to go into recovery. I spoke to his aunt and realised how they were in chaos like our home had been. Alcohol quickly changes everything and I was so glad that I was out of it and it wasn't my responsibility any more. Charles went into recovery. I spoke to Louise who I really liked and she told me he was doing well. She told Charles he had to be sober for a year before she would live with him again as she had a teenage daughter who was scared of him. Charles started drinking again and they split up as he started seeing someone else.

Charles's aunt and family said they now understood why I had left him and, without Louise around, the stable environment for Andrew had gone. I wrote to Charles and said if he took a breathalyser at the Contact Centre and passed then he could take Andrew for an extended time. He agreed and it was gradually extended. Charles had another girlfriend, Sue, who he moved in with early in 2005.
At the beginning of 2006 Charles refused to take the breathalyser anymore. Andrew was now 7 and becoming more anxious. He was fine with Charles and seemed accepting of Charles's behaviour. Andrew didn't sleep well, he had to have all the lights on and I had to sleep with him upstairs. One time he went for weekend contact with Charles and Sue, they were drunk and argued so loudly a neighbour called the police. Andrew was brought back to the police station to meet me.

Andrew didn't want to talk to Charles or see him but in 2007 I arranged for Charles and Andrew to have contact in the Contact Centre. I was called a few times when Andrew was with Charles as he wanted to come home. He was anxious about each meeting and eventually I got him some help with counselling. Andrew wasn't sleeping until 1am and I was exhausted, it was like having a new born baby.

In 2008 I stopped Andrew seeing Charles until he had a regular sleep pattern, Andrew improved although he was still very clingy. Charles and Andrew would speak on the phone but Charles was drinking and Andrew got upset. For two years they had no physical contact and in 2010 Charles wanted contact and we went back to Court. Andrew told the Court that he didn't want to see or talk to him and just have letters. The last time we heard from Charles apart from Christmas presents and a card was 3 years ago. Andrew went to Secondary School and his confidence improved once he stopped seeing Charles.

I am grateful that Andrew is healthy and I have my house and animals. I have a lot of lovely things but I can't enjoy them. I find it difficult to let go of things and have still kept all the papers that prove what happened. I am grateful that Charles was an alcoholic or I wouldn't have found Al-Anon which has been a huge factor in my survival. As bad as my experiences have been, there have been things that I could laugh about. People might think that is weird but being able to laugh kept me sane. At Al-Anon there is a lot of laughter in the room. If I hadn't had those experiences I wouldn't know how far I had come. It has allowed me to see things again, appreciating nature and being around my horses and caring for them. My confidence has gone down over the years. I have often felt that I didn't fit in and I still don't really know where I fit in now. I think that if you don't have the dips you won't necessarily have the highs as you won't have something to compare it to.

I would like to be with somebody but fear things not working out. I don't drink much myself but when I am round a lot of alcohol, as long as it's not affecting me, that is fine. I couldn't be around someone who was an alcoholic. I know I am like my Dad and I think people will see me as being quite masculine. I find it hard to believe when people tell me that I'm lovely.

I don't want to do internet dating and I don't get any offers although people think I do. I have only slept with three men in my life and I feel scared of meeting someone. I don't come across men who I like the look of. I think it's important to be attracted to someone but I'm worried I will choose the wrong kind of person.

I couldn't invite anyone back to my house which is in a mess. It's a lovely safe house but there is no space for someone else. I find it difficult to have people coming into the house and I know that having the clutter is subconsciously not letting people in. I don't dare to dream, I still live one minute at a time. Living in the moment was the way I coped with living with an alcoholic and I have trouble planning things. I can't imagine being with someone else as I still don't know me.

I would advise someone in a similar situation to mine to get in contact with Al-Anon. It's about being heard and is a blueprint for every aspect of your life. It explains so many things about yourself. You might hear things that strike a chord and help you. Going to Al-Anon allowed me to make decisions and take responsibility for myself.

I would also say AA open meetings are good to go to as you hear the alcoholic tell you things that your own alcoholic can't tell you. Al-Anon is not about the alcoholic, it is about your own recovery. There is no religion or leader and it puts things into perspective in a rational way.

Being out in nature and learning from it opens my eyes and has really helped. I have found dance helps to make me feel alive, going to dance classes or out dancing. I have learnt to be in awe of the things that are free - a great sunset makes me feel good.

Chapter 15: Mark

I met Ruth 25 years ago when we were both sixteen years old and part-time employees. We started going out locally on a Saturday night to the cinema, parties, etc. She was a typical teenager and so was I. She drank alcohol but there were no signs that she drank a lot.

The first year was normal relationship fun but after a year we split up. She instigated this and we went our separate ways. A year later we met again when we bumped into each other and started seeing each other again. Ruth became a regular customer where I was working part-time and eventually I called her. Things went fast, we were very serious about each other and after eighteen months got engaged when we were 20 years old.

Ruth quickly became pregnant with our oldest son - I think it was an accident rather than pre-meditated. James was born and when he was eighteen months old we married. We had little money and ended up living in a homeless shelter as there was no council housing available. We lived in a single room for six months and then were given a house where we lived for three years. After that we were able to afford to buy our own house where I still live.

We were both working parents and James was brought up predominantly by Ruth's parents. They did all the running around for a total of 7 years and then her father died of cancer when our second child Jeff was a year old. Her father played a big part in Ruth's life but her survival instinct made her look after the child rather than grieve her father's death. I've been told this may have been the starting point to her becoming dependant on alcohol.

Ruth's mother is very independent and had her own mother living with her. Her mother said she wanted to scatter the Father's ashes in the Black Mountains as that was his wish but she went alone and wouldn't take Ruth with her which really upset Ruth.

Ruth's father was a very dominant person and if he were to behave today as he had then, it would be classed as abuse. As a child if Ruth didn't do as she was told he would spit on his hand and slap her on the legs.

Ruth carried on working, bringing up the kids and didn't grieve at all. A couple of years later small things started to happen; the first was poor financial control. I would give her money to put away for a holiday or car. When I asked her to withdraw the money to buy a car there was nothing left in the bank account.

At this time I applied for a new mortgage and it was turned down. I eventually found out that we had been refused due to Ruth having CCJ's (County Court Judgements) for non-payment of bills. I had no idea this was going on. We shared the bills and had always done so. Once she stopped work to look after the children she had insisted that she still pay half and put accounts for utilities in her name when we moved into the new house. She hid all the letters to do with banks/bills and as everything was in her name they wouldn't speak to me directly. To negotiate the cheaper mortgage Ruth had to sign a document relinquishing her right to any equity in the house so that the CCJ's could not be linked to the mortgage.

We had our second child, Jeff, a year after moving into the new house. Ruth had two years off to look after him and then went back to working part-time.

Eleven years later I rushed Ruth to hospital with what I thought was appendicitis. I was yelling for help and was thrown out of the hospital for shouting. I sat on a park bench outside and an hour later a doctor came out, shook my hand and said "Congratulations. You've got a son". He said it in a positive manner. It took me an hour to calm down and catch my breath. Ruth and baby Adam were taken by ambulance to another hospital. I called my parents and they were as shocked as I was. Ruth is size 12 and 5'10" tall and she did not look pregnant, Adam weighed 5-lbs. and was one month premature.

I don't feel she could have carried a child for eight months after already having had two other children without knowing she was pregnant and yet managed to keep it a total secret. When we arrived at the hospital my mother asked what we were going to call him and Ruth said the name Adam immediately. I think she knew and had already spent time thinking about his name. Ruth stayed in hospital for two days and I was irrational. I lost my temper at work after an hour and disappeared for a week and stayed at home.

It wasn't in my life plan to have another child and I had wanted to travel and explore the world by now. Three weeks before Adam was born I had bought a motor home to enable us to go away on holidays as a family. I stayed at home and had to get my head into gear as to where my life was going. When Ruth came home I didn't confront her. I didn't gel with Adam until he was about 18 months old as I felt he had ruined my life. Ruth felt she had no support from me. She would have been drinking during the pregnancy as they found that her placenta had died due to excessive drinking and she had to be operated on to remove it. The doctor didn't really explain that but it was afterwards when I read up on it that I realised what had happened.

Adam has behavioural difficulties and at three years old didn't talk much and used his hands in sign language. He gets very frustrated. A child born from an alcoholic mother can be autistic but I'm not sure if this is the case or if he was not getting any attention during the day. When I came back and asked her how her day had been she spent a long time talking about all that Adam had done wrong and how difficult he was. I asked him to draw me a picture one day and that evening when I asked how he'd been she said he'd been well behaved. He'd had some attention and been busy and it also took her mind off his behaviour as she'd been doodling with him.

After Adam's birth I told Ruth I was going to go to family planning and be sterilised but I never did. I kept telling myself that I had to go but didn't like the idea. When Adam was born I put my foot down and told her she ought to stay at home and be a full time mother rather than dropping them off at her mother's.

Our fourth son, Luke, was born just over two years ago and was unplanned. When I found out that Ruth was pregnant with Luke I didn't really react. I didn't shout and go off the rails and I now believe that both of these children were a cry for help. When she was five months pregnant I noticed a bump. I joked about it initially and asked her to get a pregnancy test and she told me it was negative. I didn't believe her, bought a kit and sat with her while she did the test which proved positive.

The doctor told me that Luke was struggling when she got to eight months. She'd been for a scan two weeks previously and they said the heart beat was too strong. When a baby is in a fight for survival mode the baby takes energy away from other parts. The doctor told us they thought the baby would be better off out of the womb and induced the birth. Luke was born as a routine birth and Ruth had to be operated on again to remove the placenta which they found was rotten. Luke didn't seem to have suffered as at fifteen months he was already walking, talking and large - unlike Adam. Luke's development has been normal despite experiencing the same alcohol abuse during pregnancy that Adam had experienced.

We then continued what I thought was normal life and it was only after being in the house for eleven years that I found out what was going on. I was giving her money for housekeeping and a large amount of it was going on alcohol. She has never told me what was actually happening and kept it all a secret. When we were in our twenties and thirties I didn't think anything of it. Now I look back and realise that it was gradually creeping up and increasing.

I think there has been a serious problem for the last 8 years which started when she was 33. As a couple we've always drank socially. I can think of so many situations when she had friends around in the garden and she was drinking and they hadn't drunk anything. She would be stumbling around and deny she'd had anything to drink. She lost all of her friends because of it.

Eight years ago we bought a boat and would spend the weekend fishing, seeing friends and drinking. I stopped drinking when I kept seeing her getting drunk. I was embarrassed by her behaviour as she was drunk so regularly. I sold the boat after 3 years. I stopped drinking on the boat as it wasn't safe. She wouldn't stop drinking until she fell over unconscious. We didn't socialise with that group of people any more. They were professional people, business owners, even a headmistress who was a silly drunk.

After this we didn't socialise at all. Our joint friends didn't invite us around any more and she has ended up with no friends and is a lonely woman. I have one good male friend who has helped me through all of this.

Eight years ago I finally started seeing things clearly when I realised she was drinking during the day, Monday to Friday. I went to the kitchen cupboard where the oven cleaner, etc. were kept and found a bottle hidden there. If I got back home and she was drunk I would search everywhere for empties. I would find bottles hidden in the kid's toys, crib, all over the place.

If she wasn't at home I would pour any alcohol down the sink or leave it in a prominent place so that she could see we had found it and notice it but she would just hide the bottle again. My 21 year old son is quite outspoken and would confront her as since he was 13 he has seen her drunk on a regular basis.

When Adam was a baby she would say she had to put him to bed upstairs. She would be up there for a couple of hours and I would go up and find her drunk. When she started doing this with Luke I put my foot down and went upstairs to bring her down. If the baby cried later she would take the opportunity to get back upstairs and stay there until I went up to bring her down again. She drank vodka, beer, cider and wine. She can drink two litres of boxed wine in a day or three litres of 8% cider in a day which is the equivalent to fourteen pints of ale. When she is drunk one of her eyes becomes droopy and I could tell as soon as I got home.

Two years ago she confronted me and aggressively told me to hit her. I walked away and went to see her mother who was not surprised. She said "Oh, her as well". She promised to talk to Ruth and find out what was wrong in her life. She called me a week later and said "It's alright. I've sorted it out, she's bored!" Ruth's Mother told me that Ruth's father and her half-brother had drunk heavily. Her brother had been married for two years and suddenly got divorced and Ruth's mother inferred it was due to alcohol. Ruth's mother didn't help or solve any problems.

I didn't tell anyone except my best male friend whose mother had died of alcoholism so he is sympathetic as to what I've been through. His mother kept it a secret from his father and it was only the Coronary Report that told him. He had seen Ruth drink a great deal when we socialised so it wasn't a big surprise when we spoke about it.

I told Ruth she needed help and not long after telling her mother about Ruth's problem with alcohol it was Jeff's 18th birthday. Ruth was drunk before we even got to the restaurant and after we ordered food she fell asleep at the table. I asked for the bill without eating as I was so embarrassed. The boys ran off and spent the night at friends. I left her to it and walked home where my parents were babysitting for the two younger children. I was talking to them when Ruth got back and she staggered in. She fell over in the living room and my parents were so shocked they called Alcoholics Anonymous who advised her that it was likely Social Services would take Luke and Adam away. I asked my mother not to go ahead due to this.

About a year ago I was advised to take control of the household, including shopping so that she was unable to get any alcohol. Ruth had suggested it as a means of me starting to trust her again but it put a huge amount of pressure on me to make sure the shopping was done, kids fed, etc. after I got home from work. One day she said we needed milk and I left her money. I knew it was too much and when I came home she was drunk. It was the first opportunity and she'd taken it and gone straight to buy alcohol.

Fifteen months ago I walked out and lived in the camper van. I went to a solicitor and said I wanted a divorce. She asked me about my children and said she had a duty of care and would have to inform Social Services. I asked her not to and based on the fact that our son James and his girl friend were responsible adults in the house she agreed not to inform them.

I spent four weeks in the motor home and it took that long to see a counsellor who I found on the internet. She advised me to move back immediately and take control of the house and children otherwise she would have to make the call to Social Services. I did move back and I went to see a solicitor and spoke to my counsellor. Both advised I needed to be the responsible adult and take control of the situation.

If you had asked me a year ago I would have said I've managed to cope quite well. Once I'd been seeing a counsellor for two months I realised I wasn't coping well at all. There were some days I found it difficult to get through the day because I was so tired. A few years ago I started drinking more to be able to fall asleep. In the morning I'd start questioning myself about how much I'd drunk - not every night but every couple of months. I could be grumpy, have temper bursts, feel indecisive and I wasn't sure what decision to make. I often felt like packing the car and just leaving but knew that when I went to bed I'd be worrying about what the kids were doing and if they were alright.

My lowest point in the last few years was when I was living in the motor van and was sent a photo of my youngest son eating. That made me crash and I was ready to pack up and leave as it reminded me that I had lost them and was living in a van when I hadn't done anything wrong. I did just keep going, that's my character, I wasn't going to cave in and give up. Making sure the little ones are safe and giving them stability is what keeps me going. I don't understand how anyone can just leave their children.

When I moved back Ruth was initially pleased I was back. I put conditions in place and said she had to come clean and declare all the debts. I needed to understand whether the debts or depression came first. She agreed and I went to the van, collected my things, moved back and insisted we discussed it that evening. She gave me sufficient information that evening that she believed would stop me asking more. I gently kept asking for more information over the next few weeks and little things came out. She said she had told me everything but I knew all the information hadn't been declared as things had gone missing in the house, such as kid's toys, birthday presents, sat nav system, binoculars, etc. I discovered that the sat nav, worth £500, had been taken to a pawn shop where she got £28 for 120% interest. She admitted she had used that money to buy beer.

I offered to pay off all the debts she had created in return for her getting some help - she did go to the GP who instantly put her on anti-depressants. I was horrified at the process she went through to get those drugs. There was no counselling, she had no warning that the drugs would take about a month to work and that they shouldn't be mixed with alcohol. The renal gland releases drugs into your body to get a balance of chemicals and drinking excessively when taking the drugs immunes the renal gland so that the alcohol prevents the drugs working.

She was contacted by an NHS talk group by letter which had a questionnaire asking her about her drinking habits. She had a 30 minute telephone interview to establish whether she qualified for treatment. She was given an appointment for a 30 minute face to face interview which she didn't turn up for. She told me she had taken the kids to her Mothers who I called and asked how they were but they weren't with her. When I came home and asked Ruth how it went, she said it had been fine. She started changing her story once I asked more questions. She had two other appointments which she also failed to attend.

I saw her progressively getting worse. I am sure it was based on depression and she prescribed alcohol for herself. I regularly got home and she had made no effort to prepare anything for dinner. I don't mind cooking but I would get back and she'd be sitting in the kitchen, saying she was tired and sometimes went to bed at 8pm. She sometimes fell asleep putting the children to bed at 7.30pm and was out cold for the night. I don't know whether the sleepiness was due to alcohol or the drugs.

On several occasions I found hidden empty bottles. One time she had one full bottle of vodka in an afternoon which she denied and said she had poured it down the sink. I found the receipt that showed it had been bought that day and she'd hidden the empty bottle at the bottom of the pram. The constant lying eroded any sense of trust. I couldn't give her access to bank accounts or any money because she may have spent it on drink. She asked me not to give her money. I couldn't do the shopping, look after the kids and work 60 hours a week. I felt worn out and deflated and decided to employ someone to do some of the office work to take the pressure off me.

I started to drink more myself - away from the home. My favourite relaxation time was Sunday afternoon when I used to have a drink. I stopped having one as I realised it wasn't fair to have a drink when I told her she shouldn't drink. I started feeling guilty if I did drink.

I called Al-Anon and spoke to a lady who told me her experiences of living with an alcoholic for eighteen years. Her opinion was that alcoholism is an illness and you can live with an alcoholic. She told me it was unusual for a man to be phoning and this worried me. When you think of a stereotypical alcoholic you think of a man. I was invited to a meeting to meet all the other ladies but I didn't find the idea very inspiring.

Personally the 'illness' label doesn't add up for me and I told the Al-Anon lady that a friend of mine has cancer and that is an illness. He hasn't chosen to get cancer and I believe an alcoholic can decide whether to have a drink or not.

One Saturday afternoon she was cooking when she was drunk and put her hand in a hot pan of fat. I wondered what would have happened if the pan had tipped over onto one of the kids. Soon after that Ruth got drunk in the afternoon and fell down the stairs onto two year old Luke and pulled him over. Nothing was broken, he had cuts and bruises but I realised I had to do something. I contacted Social Services and went to see our GP.

It took two weeks for Social Services to come and see the whole family. We were all interviewed both in private and together. Social Services said I had to become the sole guardian of the children or they would take the children away into care under a residents order. I could dictate where the children went each day and Ruth had no say in the matter.

I went to Court but the Judge didn't make a judgement. He told me to go back to work and Ruth to go and sort herself out. Social Services were astounded at the decision. Ruth saw this as a victory and celebrated by being drunk for a week. Ruth left a message on the Social Services answer machine which clearly sounded drunk and they let me know. It took three weeks to go back to Court where we had a different judge and he awarded a three month residents order to me.

During the three months Ruth and I were meant to discuss a plan for working things out but a few days later I got back from work and Ruth was drunk and angry. She tried to pick a physical fight with me which I refused to be part of. I called the police and told them Ruth was drunk and threatening me. The Police recorded the phone call and could hear all the verbal abuse and shouting. They arrived in a few minutes and took Ruth away. They cautioned her and gave her the choice to sober up in a prison or go to her mother's, she decided to go to her mother's. I packed all her belongings and delivered them to her mother who didn't react or say anything to me. I recently found out that Ruth's brother is also an alcoholic and has spent a month in hospital due to alcohol damage.

Once Ruth had left, Social Services said well done, you've done the right thing as the children are safe now and good luck. There was no support in finding childcare or how to cope with the situation. Their attitude was that I should give up my business, sign on the dole and stay at home with 2 year old Luke, 4 year old Adam and 15 year old Jeff.

When I got the residents order I got my mother to take the children to a nursery and register them. I discovered the children had not had regular health checks, weren't registered with a dentist and weren't registered in any playgroups or schools. I had assumed this was being done by Ruth whilst I was at work. Through the playgroup they carried out tests for foetal alcohol damage on Adam as he was still hardly speaking. The tests showed that he was behind in progress but hadn't been affected by alcohol. His school teacher has been amazing and after 6 months at school he is a chatterbox! I am beginning to understand the affect her drinking was having on the children. If a parent is not interacting, educating and looking after them properly it has a huge negative impact.

My parents have helped a lot. It's an early start to get Adam to school and Luke to my mums. I try and get to work by 10.00 am but it's a tight squeeze. Mum collects Adam from school, feeds both the children in the evening and helps Adam with reading and counting. My parents are seventy years old and I know this isn't a long term solution.

There has been a huge improvement in the atmosphere in the house. Jeff now comes home in the evening and he is so much more relaxed and happier. He hadn't wanted to be with his Mum as he had watched her getting drunk and using money for that rather than spending money on things for the family. He used to be out in the evening, riding around on his push bike.

Ruth needs to sort herself out so that she can help look after the children. She has the boys from Saturday morning to Sunday afternoon. As her mother is in the house she is deemed to be the safe adult. At first Ruth was very angry and she now goes to classes a few times a week with Addactions. She is now admitting alcohol is a problem but has been taught that alcoholism is an illness so she is not taking responsibility for her actions. She tells me she wants to get better, find herself and rebuild her life.

After Ruth was arrested I started divorce proceedings. I have offered her joint parental responsibility on the grounds that Social Services are happy that she has made suitable progress. I have offered her contact with the children half the week. Jeff won't go to see her and my eldest son, James who is 21, also has no interest in going to see her. Luke and Adam tell me they don't want to see her.

Addaction have told me that she is not drinking any more. They breathalysed her during the day but this will only show whether someone has had a drink in the last three hours and she could have been drinking the night before or go on a bender after the meeting. Addaction have asked me to pay £1,000 for her to have a hair strand test which would show how much she was drinking and for how long. I've refused to pay for this as I don't think it will help and I'd rather spend the money on the children.

The children are now very close to me. We've really bonded and it wouldn't be constructive for them to be taken away from me. I have been legally advised that despite all her alcohol history she could come back home and step back into my life and have me evicted from the home.

The law doesn't allow for men in my situation. Social Security told me that I was a one-off situation and that most men would have just walked out and left. I believe the money that comes into the home is for the children and I'm not going to give her any. My solicitor has put forward the proposal and terms of the divorce. She's only just signed it and agreed to me being the children's full time guardian. If she wants to have the children around her she has to sort herself out. I firmly believe that a child should be able to see both parents. Adam told me recently that Mummy and Nanny drink together. What should I do? Believe a four year old child and stop them seeing her – it may propel her back into drinking again?

Despite all the anger I felt I was heartbroken because I fought that addiction with her and the alcohol won. Alcohol took my wife away. If a marriage breaks down due to a lack of love it's hard but when its alcohol it's really hard and feels like a bereavement.

The alcohol can return someone's mentality back to when they were a child and they start lying and become devious. Because of that I wasn't giving her marital attention and I had photographic evidence that she went elsewhere. She had seen several men and one time after drinking she had fallen asleep holding her mobile which showed a naked photo of herself that she'd sent to a man. I had felt something was going on as James had come home unexpectedly and found her with a man with his shirt off. Her excuse was that the dog had jumped up and she was washing his shirt. Ruth says she did it to get my attention and to make me jealous.

Since Ruth has gone I am drinking far less as I had been drinking a lot to stop me worrying over how much she was drinking. I would advise people to look at their own drinking and make sure they don't fall into the same trap. I did feel guilty as I thought I was part of the cause of why she drank but I've started to have more faith in myself.

A year ago I was in a dark place and now I feel there is a future. The marriage vows say in sickness or in health and I think you should stay together but there has to be a point when you say enough is enough and fend for yourself. You have to think of number one otherwise you'll get worn down so that your self-beliefs will be destroyed and you'll go under.

It is a chapter in my life and I'm not going to ignore it. I will learn from it and hope it makes me stronger in the future. I think there needs to be more support for families where the single parent is a man. If a father chooses to continue working to financially support his family there is no funding to help with childcare. When Ruth was still in the house, Social Services classed the children as being in protection and we automatically qualified for childcare so that Luke could go to playschool and be funded. As soon as Ruth left, this was withdrawn and once they were in my care I lost entitlement to assistance. I went to Citizens Advice and was told I was on my own and I just had to get on with it. The system is twisted as I was being encouraged to stop work and take benefits rather than work.

Seeing a counsellor and being able to talk about the situation was a great help to me. The first question I asked my counsellor what was my part in the situation; should I have done something different; what have I done wrong? She told me off for thinking it was my fault. Ruth has made choices herself. I know I work long hours and that has probably taken its toll. If I didn't work for myself and had just done forty hours a week would that have made a difference?

I have learnt that my attitude to 'fixing' a situation like this needs to change. I can't fix it and it creates depression when I realise I can't. I feel I've failed because I haven't been able to fix it. My mentality is to keep trying and I will be able to eventually change things. I finally got to the point where I accepted that I couldn't do so and needed to move on. I have learnt to understand my own actions and realise that the way I've reacted may have been wrong. I don't like confrontation whether that is at home or work and try to avoid it even if I lose money. This has happened with staff as well when rather than deal with a problem I've brushed it under the carpet.

Once Ruth's father died I think she expected me to keep her on the straight and narrow and stop her doing things she shouldn't but because I'm non-confrontational I wouldn't say anything and would let things go. I've known Ruth for 24 years and the end of the marriage has felt like a bereavement.

So much comes out of talking to people. I can't think of anything specific, it is important to start talking and not keep everything bottled up inside. I found reading 'The Curse of the Strong' was really helpful to understand the causes and the kind of people who suffer from depression. I would say be careful of advice you get from your mates. One told me to 'go off on holiday, sleep with lots of women and you'll feel right as rain'. You need sensible and level headed people around you who understand what you are doing. I don't feel judged by anyone but I do judge myself. I feel guilty, even now, just sitting here talking about it. Guilt doesn't really get you anywhere. There were good times, it wasn't all bad.

Recently I met someone and it's been a breath of fresh air to be with someone who's not drunk and wants to spend time with me, watch TV, have a meal, etc. She is making me smile again and I'm feeling much more positive. It is difficult for us to meet as she has three kids and we have two families to bring together. Usually the end of a marriage means the Dad goes off by himself and doesn't have the children. Just before I met her I felt despondent and didn't think anyone was going to want me when I've got three kids.

Long term I'd love to be with somebody and move in together. The support you give and receive as a family is something I miss. We take one day at a time and I do find it difficult to trust but can look forward to the future now.

Chapter 16: Rachel

I met Daniel when I was 24 and he was 27, he is Anglo Arab and has been in the UK since he was 16 years old. We used to go to pubs when we first dated but it was never on a regular basis. If we didn't have the money then we didn't go out and didn't drink. I only saw him drunk once when we had a party. We married about 9 months after we met and two days later we were at a dinner party and I went to make a phone call to my mother from the bedroom. One of the guests followed me into the bedroom and tried to kiss me. I told him to leave me alone and made the mistake of telling Daniel after we got home. He went mad and accused me of leading the guest on and being a slut. He said he wanted a divorce but I placated him and calmed him down. It was more than a row; it was like an earthquake and the way he treated me shattered me. I couldn't believe the man I loved was so unfeeling, unkind and distrusting of my loyalty.

After we were married he became quite controlling and if I was late home from work he would question me and accuse me of going out for a drink on the way home and chatting up other men. I think he was the one who had stopped off for a drink.

He was vile when he was drunk and was verbally abusive but the next morning wouldn't remember when I told him what he had said. He told me he would never say anything like that. The following day the same thing would happen. Eventually I started thinking I was making too much of it and that it was my problem. He only remembered what he said when he was drunk again. It was like living with Jekyll and Hyde.

He used to tell me that I made him drink. He would say "Look at what you did, you made me drink." It took me twenty years to realise it wasn't me. I felt so pathetic that I hadn't done anything sooner and for years I was angry with myself for not doing anything. On the other hand he was a real character. He was great fun to be with; he liked to be the centre of attention and was a bit of a performer; he was well read and informed; was generous to friends and had a really good heart. He told really funny jokes and then laughed at his own jokes and other people would laugh because he was laughing. He was often very flirty and if I asked him not to do it he accused me of being a jealous wife and didn't change his behaviour.

A few years after we were married we went to Kuwait to live for a couple of years. Although it is a "dry" country we made our own booze. I made strawberry wine and he made beer. We had a great social life and he started drinking on a daily basis, he didn't get drunk and didn't seem to be drinking too much.

He had work for a few years when we returned to the UK. During that time he started being very critical of me and I felt he was always getting on at me. Five years after we were married I decided that I'd had enough and told him I was leaving. He pleaded with me not to leave and his behaviour improved for a while but I think we had established a co-dependant relationship and we both thought we couldn't do without each other. Around that time I inherited a bungalow in Wiltshire and could have left him then but I did not drive, the buses were intermittent from the bungalow and I felt insecure about moving. Although I thought about it a great deal it never happened. In the end we sold the bungalow and bought a house with the proceeds which we moved into after being married for 8 years.

I started to get broody but Daniel had never wanted children. I became ill and collapsed, and my doctor who was quite intuitive told me that there was nothing wrong with me but my body was trying to tell me how strong my desire to have children was. I had tried to block it as I knew it was a difficult issue and I told Daniel that perhaps we should split up as he didn't want children. In the end he said 'I don't want to lose you so let's give it a go". I became pregnant straight away 9 years after we were married.

Daniel said this was going to be my child and I would have to do everything for it. But I felt he would be a good father and once Alex was born he fell in love with him. He was a good father up to the point of his own emotional maturity. Once Alex had grown past that point of about 7 years old and reached puberty, Daniel didn't know how to relate to him.

When Daniel had tantrums he was like a 7 year old and I think it is possible something traumatic happened to him at that age. Once Alex was a teenager their relationship broke down and though Alex tried hard, they just grew apart. I really had wanted a family life but it didn't happen. Family is very important to me and I wanted nothing more than a close-knit family unit with all members having fulfilling relationships. But alas, Daniel was not able to do this and as Alex grew up Daniel became more and more distant from his son. I have no doubt that he loved him to bits but was simply unable to express it in ways that Alex would have found emotionally connecting.

We went to Qatar for a year and I returned to the UK to have Alex and stayed with a friend. Once Alex was 6 weeks old I went back to Qatar until he was 6 months old. We came back to the UK on holiday and Daniel was called from the company that employed him and told not to return to Qatar. His work arranged for all our belongings to be packed up and shipped back to us. I never found out from him what had happened. Only recently, since his death, I found letters that showed he wasn't doing his work well in Qatar or previously in Kuwait. It must have been very stressful for him as we now had a baby. We stayed with friends and then rented as our own house was rented out. He got a job in the north of the UK and we were going to move there but he was fired after a few months. Daniel continued to have work problems throughout his life. I don't think he was drinking on the job, only socially around it but perhaps his attitude was not right as he must have been fired or made redundant at least eight or nine times.

Daniel got a job in London and started drinking more heavily. He would go to work and have two strong pints of beer at lunchtime, return to work and have two more strong pints of beer on the way home. He would come home and have two or three double rum and cokes, then two glasses of wine with dinner and a port. It was a wonder he was standing up! I usually had one drink in the evening.

He became abusive when he was drunk – that really was a bad time. A friend came down from Scotland and they got drunk together and were both verbally abusive to me. When he was sober in the morning I told him how appallingly they had both behaved and what he had said. He would deny everything, say he hadn't said it and I started wondering whether I had imagined it.

When I was 38 and he was 41 I realised he had a real problem with drink as he had been drinking for about 10 years by then. It became habitual and he drank every day. Sometimes he was as nice as pie when he came home but you never knew when he was going to explode and become abusive. He was always telling me what to do and how to do it which drove me mad. It took me a long time to realise I had to fight back and eventually I used to give him as much back and sometimes we would shout at each other. It was horrible and sometimes he would shout at me when we were out. I remember the first time that happened I got up and left. We had gone to a burger bar with our son and Daniel started criticising me so I got up and walked out. I cannot tell you the nerve it took to do that but I suddenly realised that being a decent wife did not mean I had to put up with this type of behaviour. He came running after me, apologising and I realised then that his behaviour wasn't anything to do with me.

One day when I desperately needed help to deal with his moods, drink and abusiveness, I went to the doctor, took a load of bottles and told her how much he was drinking. She told me that she couldn't talk to him without telling him that I had been to see her and I couldn't let her do that as I didn't know how he would react.

All the stress began to affect my thyroid and I was exhausted. I would take the dog out for a short walk and would wonder how I would get home. I was a nervous wreck and felt as though I was in prison and I kept thinking about how I was going to get out. I continued looking for a way out of this self-imposed prison but I wasn't making enough money to support myself. After 20 years of marriage I started re-training as a complementary therapist and I did a number of therapies.

I coped because I'm quite an optimistic person and felt I had to just keep going and couldn't let it make me sink. I wasn't really getting any support from friends as I used to cover it up and pretend everything was OK.

When I was 46 years old, I was at my lowest point and felt really desperate. Eventually I told my friend who said she realised that he had a problem but had thought I knew how to cope with it and that I was happy. I didn't tell anyone what was happening as I felt disloyal. It wasn't until 25 years into our marriage that I eventually told friends how unhappy I was and what was going on. They had seen him get drunk at parties, so they knew what his behaviour was like when he'd been drinking. He was the life and soul of a party and could be outrageous but get away with it because there was a very sweet side to him but the sweet side was not enough for me to have stayed so long.

One male friend told me that he didn't like the way Daniel spoke to me and I asked him to have a word with Daniel but I have no idea whether he did or not. My friends would tell me that they had seen Daniel during the day and he had been very pleasant. Then they would see him after he had been drinking and he was angry and had an aura of nastiness.

A pattern was established which I think was linked to work and self-esteem and instead of talking to me, he drank. Three years after being back in the UK I told him he needed to get help but he refused. One time my friend, Angela, said she would tell him off when he hadn't turned up for dinner. She thought that if someone else shocked him it may help. She told Daniel to straighten up his act and that he would lose me if he didn't. Daniel sent flowers to Angela but didn't change as he loved the bottle more.

When I was 50 I burst into tears and told my friend Angela how unhappy I was. We planned how I could leave as I didn't know how he would react. I was going to pack the car and stay with Angela's mother. I had no family as Mum and Dad had both died. The plan was cancelled when Angela's mother became seriously ill and I was unable to go and stay with her. I felt so trapped and would wake up every morning wondering how I could get out of what I felt to be a prison. My weight increased and I was very stressed, this was definitely my lowest point.

I always had to do any DIY or gardening myself as Daniel would refuse to help and would go to the pub instead. One time, when I was 52, I was painting a room and had cleared the room to get everything ready. Daniel came back home and was verbally abusive, accusing me of being destructive and destroying things. It was the last straw and I told Daniel the marriage was finished and moved out of the bedroom into the spare room. He asked me not to leave him now as Alex was doing his A level exams at school. I agreed to stay for another year until Alex had finished his exams but just afterwards, Daniel had a heart attack aged 55. When he returned from hospital I nursed him. He reduced his alcohol intake, stopped drinking spirits and ironically he became less controlling.

He had four months off work and was made redundant once he returned to work. The house was just about to be sold and he asked me to wait and not leave until he had a job. We had been married for thirty years and I agreed to wait.

He did get a job and after a year I said we needed to sell the house as I wanted to get out and knew I would become ill if I didn't leave. Early in 2005 I started to push him to resolve the situation as I was aware I would have problems getting a mortgage due to my age. I finally wrote him a letter saying I would go to a solicitor if he didn't get things moving. Eventually he decided he didn't want to move and took out a second mortgage and gave me my share of the house. I finally moved out in July after 33 years of marriage. Even till then I don't think he believed I was going to leave and it was a shock to him. He lost his job a few years later and then did some contract work and after another year I don't think he worked again. A year after I finally moved out I got a teaching qualification in a bid to earn extra money.

I felt protective of him and popped in now and then to have a coffee. When he was 65 he started to get very thin and was forgetful. I was told the forgetfulness may have been due to vascular dementure caused by drinking. Two years later we went out to dinner to celebrate Alex's birthday. Daniel became absolutely paralytic and was falling about and I was really angry with him. After dinner I didn't want to talk to him but I called Alex to ask him to phone Daniel and make sure he had got home. Alex called him and the phone was answered by a paramedic as Daniel had fallen in Euston Station. He had been taken to hospital and was later discharged at 3.00 am.

A few days later his student lodger found him collapsed at home and got him to hospital where he was admitted. They did tests and found that he had very low blood pressure so they put him through a CT scan. They found massive tumours on his liver which were secondary cancers and when they searched for the primary cancer they found this on his sigmoid colon. I visited him in hospital and was there when they told him he had cancer. He kept forgetting it which was a blessing as he didn't realise he was dying. He had bowel cancer with 80% tumours in his liver. Later that week his bowel perforated, and 8 days after admission my son and I were told he only had a week to live.

He was transferred to a hospice and I arranged for all his friends to visit him. I warned them they would be shocked at how thin he was.

He died 11 days after we were told he had cancer when he was 67 years old.

After he died I spent days crying. Although he drove me completely mad during our marriage I still cared about him. In hospital he couldn't drink and didn't seem to miss it. He was lovely, smiling and happy just like the old Daniel. Alex was amazing and spent a lot of time with him in the last ten days. He told Daniel that he loved him but Daniel never said the same to Alex and that upset me a great deal.

It all happened so fast and whilst it was a shock, I knew something was wrong with him. I always knew he wouldn't make old bones. He had a peaceful death which was good and the hospice was amazing. Alex and I were with him when he died and the nurses were so respectful. They washed him, put him in fresh pyjamas and sheets with a rose between his hands. He looked peaceful, as though asleep and it was so beautiful.

You don't realise how attached you are to someone. In spite of the difficulties there were some good times and of course we shared a wonderful son. After his death I was grieving for the sadness in his life, and for the fact that he did not have the courage or motivation to make the necessary changes in his life; for the utter tragedy of his life; the sadness that he never knew his Son as I do. I grieved both the loss of him and of the marriage. I had come from a divorced family and when I married I always swore that it would be forever.

In the last year of his life, he gave up and lived in a dirty house. In the year after I moved out he told me that it wasn't me, it was him and that he didn't understand what this life was about and found it too hard.

He was a lovely person underneath. I felt he had a beautiful soul and that is why I felt so protective of him. For Daniel, life got in the way. I think he changed once Alex was born in the early 1980's. He was about 35 when he started drinking really heavily. I don't know what happened to him as a child and whether there was a trauma. He appeared to be very confident but underneath I think he had very low self-esteem. The drinking was a way of camouflaging how he felt and the fact that he wasn't achieving in life. He died with very little money which I found distressing.

Alex is what kept me going. We've always got on really well and he was a blessing. Maybe if I hadn't had him I would have left earlier, I don't know. It took me five years to leave Daniel. I was proud of myself for doing it but also angry with myself because I had waited so long. Once I had left, it was a relief as I had enough money and could cope. It was a new start but I am still angry as I wouldn't have financial problems now if I had left earlier. When you're young you still have the time to make up for your mistakes. I'm now in my sixties and getting a job is very difficult. I feel as though I've become invisible, despite having a lot of skills.

I have learnt that I can survive financially although emotionally it has been very tough. I never expected to be in my sixties and not have enough money. I wouldn't wish my experience of living with an alcoholic on anyone. I would advise someone that if you see the early signs then get out of the relationship or live separately so that you have your own space and are not completely controlled. Make sure you leave the minute you can leave and don't have any qualms about getting all the help you need from Social Services or anyone else. Don't get into the situation I am now in where I don't know if I'll have my own home in the future because I left it too late.

I would say take as much support as you can get from friends – tell them what is going on and don't hide it. If you're in an abusive situation, get out and go to a refuge. Change your life and get out. You are much stronger than you realise you are and you are strong enough to make the changes you need to make in your life. The other thing that is really important is to be able to distance yourself from the alcoholic's behaviour. You are not responsible in any shape or manner for the drinking. Once you realise that and are able to distance yourself, then you'll be able to leave.

I've been on my own now for eight years. I would love a relationship but would have to be very sure that none of the same problems would reoccur and that the person would allow me my own space. Most of all I would need to be sure that I can communicate how I feel and be heard. The key thing is to be able to communicate - anything can be overcome if you can communicate.

To those who find themselves in the same position, I have learned:-

> That partners of alcoholics often sacrifice themselves 'to make the person 'better'.
>
> That it takes time to disassociate the alcoholic's behaviour from being 'caused' by you. That ultimately you are not responsible.
>
> That you did not pour the alcohol down their throat - that is their choice and their choice only.
>
> That you need to use every resource out there to remove yourself from the situation – social services; key workers; benefit; refuge. It takes time to re-build a life – you need to do it now. Don't wait until you are nearing 60 years old as I did.
>
> The love of friends and family will get you through.
>
> That being on my own is fine, I can do what I want, when I want, with no one to answer to. In spite of uncertainty I am happier now than I have ever been, I am optimistic and believe that life brings you what you need, when you need it.
>
> My faith in God, the Universe, call it what you want, has helped me get through the difficult times.

Would I have not had the relationship? No, I would not change that as I would not have had my wonderful son. But I should have left earlier and perhaps that would have effected a change in Daniel's life too.

I wish everyone who finds themselves in the same position as me, peace of mind and heart and that they be blessed with wonderful friends to help them away from this difficult road and onto a calmer, more peaceful path.

Chapter 17: Anna

I met Mike at the pub. I was new to the area and was taken there by a friend. Mike was there with a friend and feeling sorry for himself as his marriage had just ended. There was an instant attraction and he was terribly charming. He was in the army and came back to the area at weekends. We went into a relationship instantly and he stayed with me at weekends. He was charming to my children Sarah and David and got on well with them. He was kind to animals, Sarah loved him and David was interested in the army.

I realised fairly early on that he drank a lot. A bottle of wine went very quickly and he constantly topped up my glass. I would feel terrible in the morning after 3 bottles of wine had been drunk between us. The army culture is that it's considered big and manly to be a heavy drinker. Whilst he was away on tour he couldn't drink and then drank very heavily at the weekend. There were stories of officers drinking their entire pay packet in a weekend.

My drinking increased when he was around as he would open a bottle of wine at 3pm. He could drink 3 to 4 bottles of wine a day. He drank at home and didn't go out drinking very often. He drank a lot at the officers' mess and his bar bills were very high even though bars are heavily subsidised. I never thought of him as an alcoholic. I was used to heavy drinking because of my father and I always thought of it as manly. My father was a sober drunk and you wouldn't know that he was full of booze. He was always terribly angry and anything could set him off. Mike was the same and very unpredictable.

Until I was 12 my father worked from home and didn't drink much. He would come home and already have been to the pub across from where he worked. I know he spent many afternoons in the pub, came home and have a few whiskeys followed by at least a bottle of wine. My mother started drinking when they started to have dinner parties. She drank a lot of sherry and wine. They had screaming, shouting rows that were probably fuelled by the booze. It seemed normal as all their friends drank a lot as well. There must have come a point when they realised they were drinking too much and influencing my brother as they started to hide it.

My father bullied my brother, Paul, who didn't stand up for himself. He picked up the 'real mean drink' attitude and my brother, in a desperate attempt to mirror my Dad, started drinking heavily although I don't know how much my parents knew he was drinking. He never really lived away from home for long. I eventually found out that he had drunk his girlfriend's money and been thrown out by her. Apparently a girlfriend told my parents he was an alcoholic and they hid it. When I found out he was an alcoholic my parents said it was an illness and nothing could be done about it. I arranged for him to go to an AA meeting and he was told they should go with him which they refused to do.

There is so much social acceptance of heavy drinking but my parents were ashamed of my brother being an alcoholic. He had been drinking heavily from 19 years old and I found out he was an alcoholic when he was 39. I didn't have much to do with him as we had never really got on. He was the apple of my mother's eye and he could do whatever he wanted. It didn't matter what he did, she compensated for my father bullying him. Paul was always ill and never ate properly but he was living off vodka.

Paul died of blood poisoning at 41 years of age as his liver and kidneys hadn't been able to cope. My mother was in denial that he had been drinking and thought he had not drunk for a year. They thought it was fine that she and my father kept drinking, knowing that Paul was an alcoholic and living with them.

My parents used to row but say 'We're drinking, having fun and enjoying ourselves'. Once Mike and I started rowing after drinking and I realised I could end up in a similar place to my parents. Mike's parents were shocking alcoholics and I think drinking like he does has to be learnt.

We knew each other for 14 months before we got married and had lived together for 10 months. I took him on holiday, paid for everything and we got on really well. My business ran into difficulties and I started drinking more as I was so stressed and he topped up my glass a lot. I realise that I was taught that if you are stressed or had a bad day at work, the way to relax or reward yourself was to have a drink. We had no arguments until a year after we got married. I was earning a lot of money and owned my house and he suddenly left the army after we were married without telling me.

After we got married I became pregnant and had a miscarriage at five months. My business suffered as I took my eye off the ball. My business partner was selling my design work behind my back and five months later the business folded. I became depressed after the miscarriage and had severe depression after the business folded. I couldn't sleep, was drinking a lot and due to money worries we rowed a lot. I started working on Mike's business and his drinking became worse.

There was a New Year's party and he was drinking so much I asked him to stop, it was a red rag to a bull. At 3 am, when everyone had left or gone to bed he sat at the table and started emptying the bottles, drinking out of the bottles. I told him to stop and that he was going to kill himself. He told me I couldn't stop him and to f--- off. I left and went home and he was so drunk he stayed there for two days and slept on the sofa. They called me to tell me he was still there and I asked if I could come and collect him. They said he didn't want to come home and he continued to drink. He didn't care what people thought but nobody saw the temper tantrums, he saved those for me and the children.

Four years after marrying I could see us going down the same road as his parents and knew it would have to end but I didn't know how I was going to get out of it. I couldn't see a way out. I was so low and depressed and didn't feel I could cope with anything. I existed, got up and worked but there was no life.

He would pour the first glass of wine at 3 to 4pm and drink two bottles. If he felt really sorry for himself he drank whisky.

One night I went to bed and was woken by banging noises at 4 am. Mike had got a friend drunk and they had drunk a bottle of Tequila between them. He had got his friend to cut his hand so that they could do a blood brothers pact. Mike burst into the bedroom and was sick all over the place. I got up and came downstairs where there was blood, Tequila and ash all over the dining room. I got his friend to bed as he could hardly stand and cleaned up the mess everywhere. I was told I had no sense of humour and that I was no fun.

If we had friends round for dinner and some of them left, Mike would keep the remaining friends up until 4 or 5am drinking. I think it has a lot to do with his mother and father who were big whisky drinkers and I've been told they were always drunk. A year later he started to be away a lot on business and for long periods of time, sometimes as long as 8 weeks. He would Skype me and be angry and abusive. I think he was still drinking when he was away and I used to dread speaking to him and got used to him not being here. When he came back he would be straight into the routine of drinking heavily from 3pm onwards. He drank so much his face was bright red all the time and he would smell of booze at night in the bedroom.

About 9 months later he had a 9 week trip and when he came back he told me he had been offered a job in Europe as an employee. I pointed out that he couldn't walk away from his business and the people who had invested in it. He was angry, nasty and sulky for about 3 days and started throwing things around saying he felt trapped. I think he wanted me to throw him out and blamed me and the kids and said it was all our fault. After 3 days I told him he had to go. It was like living with a large drunken toddler who had no self-control and who you couldn't reason with.

From the time he had left the army when he became angry he would smash things. He threw my laptop out of the window and smashed his arm; he broke doors; pulled them off the hinges or would break the lock. He would go into a room and barricade himself in with furniture to prevent me from talking to him. He once slept in the garden for 3 days with a sleeping bag and refused to come into the house which was really embarrassing as the children had friends around.

Sometimes he would have a tantrum and literally throw himself on the floor, kicking his heels and biting his fists as he was so angry. You never knew when it was going to happen and I would be told it was all my fault. It was such hard work and I can't believe how exhausting it was but how you get used to it. I felt totally responsible because I had been told so many times that it was my fault that I had finally believed it.

I drank too much during that period. I didn't realise at first as he was always topping me up. My tolerance for alcohol is far lower but it takes a long time to recover from the experience of living like that. It took me 2 years to recover and it is only now, after 3 years, that I feel healed.

I knew once he had gone that I would implode and I did. After 2 months I was agoraphobic, paranoid, and physically ill, all at the same time – I was a mess. I had hormone problems as well after the miscarriage. My doctor was brilliant. It took 16 months before I felt I wasn't depressed anymore and didn't blame myself for everything. I have learnt a lot and will not allow men, even friends, to treat me badly. I think I have been attracting men who think I am second rate and if I did anything well they would get angry.

When Mike got angry and we rowed he frequently pushed me over with the intention of hurting me. If I was hurt he would tell me to stop being a drama queen and that I was making it up. One time I put my arm up to stop him hitting me. He broke my wrist by hitting it. He grabbed the side of my hand, crushed it and broke two fingers. My bone was sticking up on my arm. He told me it was broken and I could get myself to hospital – of course it was all my fault.

I thought if I stood up for myself he wouldn't do it to me again. But that is not what happened. If I fought back he would hit me harder and he almost wanted me to fight back so that he had an excuse for hitting me harder. After he had broken my arm I knew I had to get out of the situation but didn't know how. Once I knew he was going away on business I was so relieved. I don't think that he cared about being violent as the army culture he was used to meant violence was normal.

When I had asked him to leave he said, as long you remember you threw me out. The instant relief for me and the children was great. His behaviour helped me get rid of him when he found someone else who would financially look after him and he demanded to have all his things. The children went through the house and filled about thirty bin bags. My son called Mike's father and asked him to come and collect them. My son had been angry with Mike and one time had gone for Mike, shouted at him and grabbed him by the throat.

When you're in the situation you don't realise how bad things are. If you're told that it's your fault all the time then you will believe it and think it's up to you to fix it. Now I know I should have got out sooner and I know what to look for. My lowest point was after the miscarriage and then after he had gone. I had coped for 4 years and kept going but once it stopped I just collapsed. I was still being told by Mike and his father that the end of the marriage was all my fault and I had ruined it.

A few months after I met Mike, his mother died. His parents had a huge row when his father hit his mother and then went to the pub. When he came back he found her dead from an overdose of pills and whisky which had caused a heart attack. I have seen Mike's father angry - he had no respect for women and told me I knew nothing and should keep quiet. If Mike saw his parents as role models, this is where he learnt to drink and hit.

My kids kept me going. I thought this is my house and I would sort it out and felt bad that I couldn't or didn't deal with the situation quicker. My kids are angry with me for not sorting it out sooner and they are judgemental. I've learnt that I'm much tougher than I thought. For the first 18 months after he left I didn't think so and thought I would never cope or get better and move on. It teaches you a lot. What it has taught me more than anything is never to listen to someone else's opinion of yourself. Your opinion and being able to live with yourself is most important.

I think it's a women's thing – we want to be loved and put up with unacceptable behaviour and manage difficult people. The people behaving like that are the ones who are telling you you're rubbish. All your insecurity is based on what other people have put onto you. It is an epiphany when you realise that other people's opinion doesn't matter. I don't care if I don't wear lipstick when I go out; if someone doesn't like the wallpaper in my house; if they don't like my attitude, lifestyle or what I read this is who I am. I am kind and know that I am OK and am content with who I am. I know I have lots of faults but I have lots of redeeming features too. I don't sit around wondering if I'm worthy anymore. If you spend your life being eaten up by self-doubt you don't get anywhere. I don't have people around who treat me badly.

I am scared of a new relationship and am not interested. I need time for myself after 20 years of looking after men. I haven't spent enough time working on myself yet and I still find it difficult going out and meeting new people but I am developing new interests.

I couldn't live with someone again. It would have to be someone extraordinary with a separate wing in a house! They would have to have a separate bedroom as I love sleeping alone. I have met lots of men and been asked out but always said no. I have good male friends but I'm not bothered. I would tell people in my previous situation to get help, get some outside support and tell them what is happening so that someone can tell you that you're not going mad. Different people have different ways of coping with things and if you're not coping, definitely get help.

I didn't talk to friends but cried all the time and people who knew me saw I was low. I blamed it on my business and the miscarriage but I didn't tell people I couldn't live with this man who was making my life a misery. I couldn't say that, people could see it was going wrong but they didn't know the real reason why I was depressed.

You find out who your friends are when you're in trouble. Be honest with people as soon as possible and be honest with your kids once you know that it's not all your fault. As I believed it was my fault I didn't feel I could ask for help. I don't know why relationships based on drink and violence take so long to break up, they should be the fastest.

Chapter 18: Jack

I met Rebecca in 1988 at work. She was my secretary and I was living with someone else at the time. Most of the office went out for drinks on a Friday night and Rebecca was dating someone on my team. She went away in 1990 for a gap year in Australia and then worked in Melbourne. While she was away her boyfriend was unfaithful and I told him that he had a few weeks to tell her when she returned or I would tell her. He didn't tell her and the relationship ended after I told her what was going on.

I was now living on my own and Rebecca came back to work with us in 1991. I invited her to a charity ball with other friends and we stayed in a hotel. We then started going out. Our relationship developed quickly and she moved in after about 10 months. She moved offices to another firm and I was considering a job offer in Australia.

Rebecca was unable to get back into Australia due to having had a gap year there. We got married in 1992 to enable her to go to Australia but the job I had been offered fell through. I found work in London again, Rebecca also changed jobs and we rented a flat as ours was already rented out. Three years later I was headhunted and the opportunity came to work in South Africa and we went to live there in 1995.

Rebecca was a 'capable' drinker. She drank a lot but not excessively. The office used to bring a drinks trolley around at 4 or 5pm and it was the norm to spend the evening drinking – there was definitely a drinking culture in my work world. Thinking about it now, there was some culpability on my part as we rented a flat within easy distance of Soho so we could get home easily. What I first began to understand when we went to see her relations was that they had a very rigid drinking routine. They drank at weekend lunchtime from 11.30am and weekdays would start the evening with a large gin and tonic.

Her father was ex-military and was in charge of mixing his own drinks with large measures. He had early onset of Alzheimer's in his 40's. Rebecca's older brother was living in the States but when he got back it was clear that he had a drink problem. Rebecca's uncles and great uncles had been alcohol dependant and drank the family's fortune. They had owned a brewery and football club which had to be sold to pay off their debts.

We lived in South Africa for 5 years. Initially I went there on my own for 6 months and found a house whilst Rebecca finished work on a project. South Africa has a drinking culture – it is so hot, you have a soft cold drink or beer in your hand a lot of the time. We settled into life there and started socialising. The South Africans are very relaxed and you would turn up for lunch at 2.00pm and not eat till 6 or 7 pm and in the meantime you would be drinking. We both drank and I wasn't aware of how much she was drinking. She became pregnant in 1998 but didn't drink at all during the pregnancy.

Drink-driving in South Africa is the norm and is almost the national sport. A neighbour came to the door one day and asked if we knew where his Porsche was. It turned out he had been drunk, crashed on the highway and they found it on the roof! I was offered a brandy at a breakfast meeting once by a client!

Rebecca had our daughter Elizabeth in 1998 and went back to work when Elizabeth was 3 months old. She enjoyed her work and they had an in-house bar on a Friday night. She would leave her car there and I would collect her. We had a wonderful woman who looked after Elizabeth and who babysat if we wanted to go out. Rebecca missed her family network, despite having help with Elizabeth and wanted to go back to the UK.

My Dad had a stroke in 1999 and Rebecca's mother was struggling health-wise. We came back to the UK for Christmas and decided to move back for good. I went back to South Africa for three months for my resignation period. We bought a house in London that we refurbished and we both found work. We found a childminder for Elizabeth who was really good.

Rebecca's brother, Rupert, was back in the UK as well and flying commercially. We visited him regularly in the country. I started to notice that Rupert drank a lot of vodka for breakfast. When we came back from South Africa in 2000 and visited him I could see that his drinking was a problem. He frequently complained of having a bad stomach but never seemed to eat anything. He had huge bottles and cans of cider, vodka and wine. We always bought food with us to cook as he didn't have much in the house.

After 2 ½ years things came to a head. We came to see him one Friday night to a dark house and found him passed out on the bed, fully dressed. He eventually came to the door to let us in and hit and cut his head on the door frame. About this time he lost his job and I said to Rebecca that he needed help to sort himself out. Rebecca gave a few excuses about his health and being troubled but refused to see that it was serious. 18 months later Rupert told us he had sold his van but we found out he had crashed it. The same thing happened to his car and he lost his licence. His house had to be sold as he couldn't afford to live there.

During this time I was doing up our house and often working away from home. Elizabeth went to the local primary school and Rebecca was working full time. One of my business partners was spending £5,000 a month on beer and curries. He was going through a divorce and miserable but I told him it had to stop. At the same time I realised that Rebecca was spending a lot of money as I was doing the accounts. We were considering putting Elizabeth into a private school and I was assessing whether we could afford the fees. There was a hole in the accounts. She was always buying a lot of shoes but I realised that was not what she was spending money on.

Rebecca bought her first moped as it was the best way to commute and she was stopping off at an off-licence to buy wine and gin. Occasionally I used her moped to go to the gym and often discovered cigarettes and half a bottle of gin in the carrier. With the stress of moving back to the UK Rebecca started drinking more and we rarely had sex unless she had been drinking a lot. She often went to bed early after supper and our sex life ceased at this point. We really weren't getting on in 2006.

I had to do business socialising a couple of nights a week and I didn't know if she felt abandoned. She filled her own glasses regularly throughout the week and was drinking a bottle of wine every night. I told her it wasn't a good idea at which she got angry and stormed off saying it was none of my business.

In 2008 three generations of her family drove to France for a holiday for two weeks where we had 5 gites. There were 25 of us and it was clear that most of them were drunk most of the time. I organised the food and cooking and there was some serious drinking going on. I had to return to London for a three day business trip and when I got back I realised that Rebecca was drinking a great deal. She started drinking in the middle of the morning and I realised her laugh soon changed and became quite manic and she often seemed clumsy. She had gained weight over the previous 2 years and I remember thinking that this is not the person I married.

The recession started to affect my business and there always seemed to be less money in the account than I thought there should be. After the holiday in France we descended into a period of madness and disagreements. We talked about splitting up but I wanted to stay together until Elizabeth left home. We often had people round for lunch and dinner as I enjoy cooking. It became embarrassing as Rebecca was drunk before anyone arrived. On one occasion I told her to stop drinking until people had arrived and when I asked her to serve dessert it was clear she was drunk. She huffed and puffed and slammed doors and that was the end of lunch. I decided it wasn't worth having people over after that as it was embarrassing. We didn't go out together after that and were definitely going our separate ways. I was working really hard for less money as the recession had really affected work.

In 2011 I sat down with Rebecca and told her I'd had enough. She was always drunk and picking fights so that she could storm out of the room and go to the bedroom to drink. I had moved into the spare room by this stage and kept finding empty bottles in drawers in the bedroom. She had frequent motorbike accidents which she always said was someone else's fault and once ended up in hospital where she stayed for a week following an accident.

She drank a lot but was always sprightly in the morning. She would often not eat in the evening after I'd cooked and say she wasn't hungry. She then went up to the bedroom, watched TV and drank. Most days she would drink one bottle of wine and half a bottle of gin.

Last year she lost her job twice and went off the rails. I invited a relative to stay and we organised a barbeque in the summer to celebrate his birthday. Before I started cooking at 6pm Rebecca had fallen over twice and was clearly drunk and didn't eat much. We had an argument and she stormed off to the bedroom.

Next morning I was cooking breakfast and Rebecca appeared a bit wobbly saying we didn't have enough champagne for that night and was going out to get some. She had a couple of drinks that morning and we went to the pub with the relative after which we returned and I cooked lunch. She continued to drink and ended up sleeping on the sofa for the afternoon. Elizabeth told her to shut up and go to bed as she was drunk.

Rebecca was not from an affectionate family whereas I am and wanted to be affectionate but there was never an attempt to rekindle our relationship. I made an offer to Rebecca that she could keep the house but she would have to find the money for school fees. I decided I'd had enough and started to paint the house to get it on to the market. Rebecca was upset and worried about how much money she was going to get and where she was going to live. The house was sold and Rebecca has bought a house with no mortgage and Elizabeth lives with her.

Rebecca's uncle has also given her a lot of money in the same way as he helped her brother, Rupert, who has become an alcoholic. Rebecca is not working and continues to drink heavily. I see Elizabeth regularly and she walks to school. I have to send the school fees directly to the school as otherwise Rebecca would spend it. Rebecca is now drunk a lot of the time. A friend of ours is a nurse and Rebecca went to the doctors drunk after which I asked the nurse if Rebecca was capable of looking after Elizabeth and she said 'No'. I told Elizabeth to pack her bag and took her away for the night. The following day I arrived at the house to find Rebecca watching TV and I told her she had to sort herself out. I think she was scared I was going to take Elizabeth away. I told her to get professional medical help and tell her mother what was happening.

Rebecca's brother, Rupert, went into Rehab and then "escaped". He broke into his Mother's house and took the keys for a Landrover when he was drunk. The Police were called and found him unconscious in the car after crashing. He was taken to hospital where he recovered from the accident. Rebecca hasn't hit her low spot yet and I don't want it to happen when Elizabeth is in the car with her. Elizabeth has a 'grab and go' bag packed in case she needs to leave the house quickly. Rebecca says she's going to counselling but I don't know if this is true. She still isn't working.

What kept me going through the worst times was self-belief; as long as people aren't shooting at me I just carry on! Up until the end I really thought I could turn it around once Rebecca realised what she was doing. Elizabeth has also kept me going. The darkest days were from when we decided to split and were living together until we sold the house. It's difficult to deal with three generations of her family. They all want to offer their opinion and are all difficult people.

I had support from friends once I told them what was going on and that I was splitting up with Rebecca.

I've recently met someone but am not involved with them. I would like to go out with someone who isn't a nutcase or an alcoholic! I won't go to a bar to meet someone. It does seem to be a progressive illness and I wasn't prepared to wait around in a sexless, soulless marriage. I had to be selfish and get out as I had been drained by being with her for 8 years whilst she drank. What killed the relationship for me was when we came back to the UK and all the arguments started.

Turning 50 made me realise that 'No, I don't have to do this'. You do need to think about yourself and be objective, particularly when children are involved. I'm concerned that Elizabeth will feel she has to be loyal to her mother and grandmother and not tell me what's really going on. I take every opportunity to see Elizabeth and spend half term, etc. with her. It's clear there is a problem with alcohol, usually gin, right the way down the family line.

Section 4

Chapter 19: Getting help

If you imagine yourself one year from now, where do you see yourself? How will you feel and what will you be doing? If you are in an unhappy situation can you imagine continuing as you are for a further 5 years? What is your answer? Can you imagine continuing as you are for 2 years? Can you imagine continuing for another year? It is absolutely up to you and nobody else can truthfully answer these questions. If the answer to any of them is 'No' then what are you going to do about it?

If you feel that you need support then please consider what form of support would be most helpful for you. You could either refer to the contact list at the back of this book, carry out an internet search or speak to someone you trust, whether that be a family member, friend, doctor or therapist.

When people decide to talk to someone they are naturally concerned about how the other person will react, whether they will be able to communicate the problem without being misunderstood, dismissed or even ridiculed. When someone comes to see me as a Therapist my one and only concern is how I can be of assistance to that person and I listen without judgement. When you are feeling depressed or beaten down by your situation you may find it difficult to accept or believe that people do have your best interests at heart and that they will want to be as helpful as possible.

Once you realise that you are not alone and that there are people out there who will understand and empathise with you then it can be very liberating. Sharing a problem is sharing a burden and if the person you decide to speak to doesn't understand, then perhaps it would be advisable to find someone else. You may have resisted finding help as you felt there couldn't be a solution and there was no hope. If the problems have existed for a long time then they may take longer to resolve but it doesn't mean that things cannot change.

There may be occasions when someone misunderstands you and says something in response to what you have told them that you feel is inappropriate. In those circumstances it's important to clarify what they mean as their intention may have been completely different. It is said that 70% of our communication is through body language and the tonality you use rather than your actual words. It's important that you choose someone you feel comfortable with and also feel you can communicate easily with. Some therapists may use language that contains technical terms that are difficult for people to understand and it's important to be able to say that you need clarification if you're unsure of the meaning of a word.

When meeting with the person you decide to talk to it's important that you can meet somewhere private where your conversation cannot be overheard. If possible children, even very young ones, shouldn't be present as children sub consciously take in what is being said and it could be distressing for them.

If you decide to see a Therapist they should be professional and provide assurances that the discussion will be completely confidential. If you find that your needs are not being met then review what you have gained and make a decision whether to stop seeing them. It is important to bear in mind that sometimes part of a therapist's work is to help you look at things that you don't necessarily want to see, feel or hear. If you truly want to move on then you will need to make choices and decisions that may be hard but necessary. You may need to see more than one person before meeting someone that you have confidence in and who you feel can help you move on with your life.

There are many different types of therapists and it's important to find out how they work and the types of therapies they use. You also need to know whether you feel comfortable with them as the discussion will be very personal. Some people find it easier to open up to someone they do not know and who they need not see again once a series of sessions have been completed.

Some therapists offer a free half hour telephone call or face to face meeting that enables you to decide whether you could work with that person or not. Some actually provide the opportunity to work in sessions over the telephone as well as in face to face meetings which offers more flexibility. People may have a past experience that is very painful for them to discuss. They may even never have voiced it and need to feel they can trust a therapist before divulging it.

Sometimes you may decide that you want your drinking partner to see the same therapist and it will depend on the therapist themselves as to whether they feel this would be advisable. It could potentially put the therapist in an awkward situation if the partner has given intimate details that the drinker knows nothing about. Trust issues can be problematic. The drinking partner may start the session feeling that they have been accused and need to defend themselves. Starting from this standpoint will naturally affect how they perceive any response from the therapist; they may be resistant and suspicious to suggestions made by the therapist. Some couples go to joint therapy in order to discuss their situation. In this case the therapist will provide a safe environment for each person to talk about how they perceive the situation and the particular aspects of it that affect them most. The therapist will often suggest that they meet for individual sessions with each person to give them the opportunity to talk through anything they don't feel comfortable discussing in front of their partner.

When the relationship has been dysfunctional for a long period of time it is quite common for one of the couple to have sought solace elsewhere and had an affair in an attempt to have their needs met. If you feel a lack of affection or enjoyable sex and someone else shows you affection, appreciation or attention you can feel easily drawn towards them. Whilst honesty is usually the best policy, being totally honest about any affairs can have a devastating impact on the relationship and sometimes becomes the last straw.

If you want to save the relationship then it may be best to build it back up before providing your partner with information that could further reduce their self-esteem and sense of self-worth. People often have the impulse to tell all as the guilt is too much to bear; this will make them feel exonerated and relieved once it is out in the open but what effect will it have on their partner? If someone has contracted a sexually transmitted disease then for the sake of their partner's safety it is necessary to let them know in order to protect their health.

Your therapist can advise and make suggestions as to the choices that are available to you and what is very important is that they do not tell you what to do. Only you are capable of making decisions about what needs to be done and it is paramount that you come to those conclusions yourself. You may feel stuck right now and fearful of the idea of making decisions as it feels too difficult and overwhelming.

Some people I've worked with say they have no idea what they want to do and find it very difficult to make decisions. Once they relax and allow themselves to think and listen to their inner voice or subconscious mind then they find the answers come to them. Sometimes you may wake up in the morning and have clarity on what actions you need to take; sometimes it can come at an odd moment in the day or during a therapy session. What is important is that you learn to forgive yourself and remove any self-blame or criticism that has been running around in your head. We are all extremely good at accusing ourselves and calling ourselves names, criticising and repeating things we may have been told. You need to stop those voices and decide that you are not going to allow the negative thoughts, voices or actions to continue.

One thing you could do is mirror talk. Literally stand in front of the mirror and take a good look at yourself. What do you see, think, hear or feel as you are looking at yourself? If there are any negative thoughts then acknowledge them and put them to one side. Then replace that negative thought with a positive one and repeat it either in your head or out loud. Next you need to smile at yourself in the mirror which can feel strange and sometimes difficult to do, particularly if you feel that you don't have anything to smile about. What do you see, hear or feel? What thoughts, voices or images come to mind? Again you can acknowledge them, put them to one side and replace them with positive thoughts.

When I grew up I read the Mrs Pepperpot stories written by Alf Proysen, which were about a lady who would shrink to the size of a pepper pot without warning and at very inconvenient times in order to create interesting and amusing stories. Mrs Pepperpot used to give herself a good talking to in the mirror in order to encourage herself and to give her inspiration to deal with these difficult situations.

Look in the mirror and say hello to yourself and smile. Then ask yourself a very simple question. If it's the morning ask "what can I do today to make you happy?" If it's the evening then ask "what did I do well today". If you decide to do this then build it into your routine, perhaps before or after brushing your teeth, whatever works well for you? Do it for a week and see how you feel; do it for a month and see how you feel. If you have a crisis or difficult situation then go into a quiet place and talk to yourself and ask yourself the question: "what would be the best thing for me to do now?" I know the saying 'the first sign of madness is talking to yourself' but this does work!

Your intuition is an incredibly powerful tool and can assist you in comforting yourself and building your self-esteem. What have you got to lose? 'Nothing' is the answer, so go ahead, do it and if you find it better to say something else to yourself then try that too, whatever works best for you.

Chapter 20: Preparing for change

Safety

If your drinker is verbally or physically abusive and you fear your own safety or that of others in the home, then please ask yourself why you stay with your drinker. However much you have loved them or perhaps do love them, you and others in the home do not deserve to be punished for loving them. As I have already mentioned, it is important to speak to someone you trust and get help to leave a dangerous situation.

You sometimes need an objective perspective to realise that your drinker's behaviour is unacceptable and you do not deserve to be treated badly however many times you have been told that you do. The more people you tell that you are experiencing verbal or physical abuse, the less likely your drinker will be to inflict it on you. However you must be aware that in a heavily drunken state your drinker will not necessarily remember this and unfortunately the rate of injuries inflicted in domestic abuse is higher where alcohol is involved.

Your safety can also be affected if your drinker is a smoker and there is the potential that a fire could start from a dropped cigarette. If they come home late after drinking and decide to cook there is also a safety risk of fire. They may invite drinking friends home with them who you know nothing about and may put you and other family members at risk. They may leave doors or windows unlocked making you vulnerable to burglary and affecting the safety of your home and its occupants. They may drink and drive on a regular basis and take other people in the car with them whilst they are drunk. All of the above are important to consider when you are making an assessment of how alcohol is affecting you and any other family members.

Dealing with fear

Many people living with a heavy drinker will have become accustomed to an overwhelming sense of fear. It might be fear that something bad is going to happen and that nothing will go well or that something will happen to them and nobody else will look after their heavy drinker or any children they have.

The letters in the word fear have been said to represent "**F**alse **E**vents **A**ppearing **R**eal." The little voices that we all have in our head will do a very good job of escalating any fears that we have, making them out of proportion to what is reality. It has been estimated that 77% of the thoughts we have are negative ones and therefore we have to work hard at overcoming them or keeping them in check. If someone is suffering from depression then stopping the downward spiral is extremely difficult and it is unlikely that they will manage to start the process of change on their own and will need some help.

What are your greatest fears about the situation you are currently in? Take some time now to write them down and look at each one of them and analyse how realistic each fear actually is. People often find it comforting to write things down and stop the thoughts going round and round in their heads.

Some partners might be most concerned about material issues and if you work through them and think of a solution to each of the fears, then it will remove the power of that fear. There may be some that seem too great for you to think of a solution for and you may need some professional help or information from an outside source or the internet. Do whatever you can to free yourself from those fears and if you think of others in the future then simply add them to the list and go through the same process.

Once you have control over the fears that your mind conjures up then you will be less fearful of change and what that could bring.

Going through the stages in chapter 21, taking one at a time, will help to remove embedded fears that you may be unaware of.

How our mind works

It is helpful to understand how your mind works to ensure that you can make change as effective as possible. We all have two parts of our minds that we work with. The first is called the conscious mind and the second the subconscious mind. It is the conscious mind that makes decisions and plans, it makes us able to look at a situation, evaluate it and then make a judgement on how we should or could react. The conscious mind is able to look back into our past experiences and memories and imagine what might happen in the future. Our subconscious mind is responsible for everything that happens in our bodies physically such as organ regulation and function, breathing and digestion. The subconscious mind can only work in the present and is unable to look back into the past or forward into the future.

Our subconscious mind acts on autopilot and allows us to perform tasks such as driving a car without thinking about each separate task such as changing gear and allows us to listen or talk to a passenger at the same time. When something has been done many times it becomes habit and the conscious mind is then able to focus on something else. The subconscious mind deals with four million bytes of data per second as opposed to the conscious mind which processes about four thousand bytes per second.

The reason that all this information is important is that it helps us to understand why people find it difficult to change their behaviour. During our day to day lives we process most of the information we receive using our subconscious minds. The majority of the decisions we make on a daily basis are based on what our subconscious mind perceives to be true. We use past experience to create the truths or beliefs that we have. These can be what our parents taught us, our peers, teachers, and any personal experience. From the time of being born until the age of five we live subconsciously and our minds are like sponges absorbing everything. By the time we are six years old the majority of our personality is developed which means those first five years are critical to our beliefs.

You may have made positive changes in your life and become frustrated when you reverted back to past behaviours. The reason for this is that you were most likely using your conscious mind to make the decisions and try to change the subconscious mind. It does not matter how much our conscious mind wants something or knows it would be good for us, unless the subconscious mind perceives it to be true then it will not accept it and will effectively sabotage it.

Communication with the subconscious mind has to be in the present so if there is a change that you want to make then you have to imagine that it is true, has happened and is therefore in the present. This can seem like a very strange thing to do as you may almost feel as if you are lying to yourself.

As we become adults we start to question things more and develop a system of filtering where we decide if something is true or not and then pass the information onto our subconscious mind as the truth. In order for us to access the subconscious mind and instil new positive beliefs we have to bypass the filter system and the best way to do this is to become open minded and think like a child again. I do not mean that you have to become childlike but as children we took facts that were given to us and emotionally and intellectually accepted them. You need to be able to imagine what you would like to be your reality and imagine it exists now in the present using all your senses.

This may sound completely crazy but it works. It can work on small desires or goals such as being seen as confident and composed when going to an interview for a job and larger desires such as wanting to be in a positive relationship. By repeatedly visualising what we want and telling ourselves that we already have it and it's in the present then the subconscious mind will perceive it as reality and it eventually becomes reality. Repetition of the visualisation is very important as it creates a habit; it generally takes thirty days for a behavioural change to become a habit and accepted as normal behaviour. The more engrained a negative habit is then the longer it may take to change that particular habit. The goals or changes that you want to make maybe short term or long term.

Belief

Do you believe that you have choices and opportunities? Do you believe in yourself? Do you believe that you are capable of making decisions and bringing about change in your life? The more we believe something the more certain it becomes and the more it is likely to happen. If you feel certain that something is possible for you, your belief will become stronger. Likewise the more you feel doubt and question your beliefs the more likely you will start to disbelieve and ultimately kill a belief.

We can change our beliefs whenever we want and beliefs are one of the few things in our lives that we can truly control. Your beliefs will shape your actions, how you behave and what you decide to spend your time on. Beliefs will create results from your actions and they will create your circumstances – how, where and with whom you live your life.

Many of us will believe that once we are living in a large house or have our dream car or partner then we will feel happier and enjoy life more. We believe that the results are what create positive feelings and whilst this can happen, if we are constantly feeling we are inadequate, are hoping and looking towards the distant future, then we may be unaware that our day to day beliefs and actions are affecting our long term future.

Things that happen to us today, tomorrow or next week will affect us negatively, positively or not at all. You will feel something about them and you do have a choice as to how you react and what you feel. Some would say that it is unhelpful to point this out and that if someone is seriously depressed and feels they are at a dead end then how can they decide how they react to their current circumstances? However, putting an extreme case such as this to one side and considering your own situation, do you see how the way you are feeling may be causing the results?

How would you feel if you felt more positive about your life and changed the way that you live? If feelings cause actions and actions cause results can you see the possibilities that this gives you? This is not just positive self-talk and if you can simply consider it then it may help you. If you can imagine how you would feel living in a safe warm environment or with someone who treated you well, whatever your dream or wish is, then how would that feel?

Wanting something and believing it is possible is one thing but you also have to work to make it happen. Breaking your problems down into smaller manageable chunks helps to give you a sense of perspective and make it easier to recognise when you have achieved changes in each of those areas.

The longer the patterns of behaviour have existed the longer it takes to start the process of change or to even comprehend that change is possible. The feelings of disillusionment that a partner may experience contribute to a feeling of helplessness and acceptance that this is the way things are and this is what they deserve. It's difficult to get someone in this situation to accept that they deserve better and that changes can be made to improve their lives. There is a well-known saying "If you keep on doing what you're doing then you will keep on getting the same results". Whilst the partner may have tried different approaches to discuss or change the heavy drinker's behaviour, unless they continue to seek ways to change their own behaviour first then the heavy drinker's behaviour is unlikely to change.

This is not a question of blame; partners often feel they are being blamed by the heavy drinker and by society for causing the problem. They will also hear words such as co-dependency and feel that if they ask for help they will be judged. They feel ashamed and fearful - were they the original reason the drinker started drinking and are they stupid, ugly, lazy, useless as the drinker tells them? There is also the fear that if the drinker is diagnosed as being an alcoholic what will happen then? There will be the shame and embarrassment of people finding out, the drinker may lose their job, they may not be able to pay the mortgage, lose the house etc.

The partner's primary concern will be for the welfare of any children and the family unit. If they fear the drinker may lose their job due to alcohol consumption then they are likely to call in and say their drinker is ill rather than let people know what is really going on. A partner is unlikely to call the police when they know the drinker is drink driving on a regular or daily basis for fear that they will lose their driving license and be unable to get to and from work. A partner is also unlikely to call the police if they are physically abused for similar reasons. Lying or concealing the truth for self-protection or protection of the family unit is a natural instinct that will remain in place unless they perceive the situation as reaching rock bottom and decide that they cannot continue living as they are. This could be when the partner realises that their children's wellbeing is under threat or that their own life is in jeopardy.

If you feel that your life or your children's lives are at risk then please take immediate advice and leave the dangerous situation. Change takes time and your life/lives cannot be at risk during that time.

Preparing for change

First and foremost it is really important that you take some time when you know that you will be on your own to find a quiet place where you will not be disturbed by your drinker or other family members. I would strongly suggest that you either buy or find a book that you can write in and record the exercises that you will be working your way through.

There is no need to be concerned by the word "exercise" as this will not be like going back to school. It will require some time and effort to work through the small achievable stages that are not daunting and you can achieve results. There is no such thing as failure as you will learn from anything that doesn't appear to be giving you the results that you want. You can then use what you learn, to work towards bigger changes. You have already made a large step by buying this book as you want to understand and change the ways things are and you can do this now by taking things one stage at a time.

You have read the facts about alcohol and the effects that it has on people. You will no doubt have understood some of the things that you have experienced and the effects they have had on you. The third section of the book gave you the opportunity to read other peoples experiences and realise that you are not alone and that there are other people going through the same or similar experiences as you. It also showed you how some have learnt to cope and the consequences of any actions they had taken. These will not in any way dictate that you will experience similar consequences if you undertook similar actions, as each person's situation is unique.

I would suggest reading through all of this section of the book and then going back to re-read the sections that you felt might be most helpful. There are some very varied suggestions in this section some of which will seem ridiculous, childish or obvious but they are surely worth considering and carrying out if there is a possibility they could provide a positive outcome to some of the dilemmas that you are now facing. At least they will start the shift that will allow you to become unstuck. If a change seems too huge and daunting then think about moving a few degrees as just the smallest change in you will cause ripples in the people around you and perhaps result in them making slight changes as well. Shifting half a degree a day or a week will gradually create far reaching consequences that you cannot currently imagine.

This is a long term problem that needs a long term solution. There may not be a quick result. It may well take time and in our society people are not necessarily good at accepting this as we live in an age where information and reactions to communication is instantaneous. Mobiles and the internet have completely changed how we perceive time and our expectations of getting the results or information that we want.

Please consider taking time to practice and use some of the exercises in this book and to understand that you deserve to take time out of a busy schedule to think about yourself and your needs.

One thing you need to be clear on is that your drinker will be unlikely to ever agree with you that they are drinking too much. They will probably know someone that drinks more and may forget or be in denial about how much they actually consume themselves. They are very unlikely to say "I am a heavy drinker and have a problem with alcohol". Even if they did it is not going to improve the situation or make you feel better. A confession does not necessarily result in a change in their drinking and even if they were to agree with you that they might have a problem, they may do so simply to keep you quiet and "to get you off their backs."

Often a problem drinker will say that they are not hurting anyone else without realising or accepting that they are affecting others in the household and you particularly. Your health may be suffering from anxiety, fear, lack of sleep, lack of appetite etc. but they may not acknowledge that these symptoms are due to their drinking. This can make you feel more frustrated, angry and stressed. Living with a problem drinker is very stressful; the long term effects can affect your health in other ways due to a reduced immunity to common colds or recovering from anything that you catch. Stress is often caused by the uncertainty of a situation and when you live with a problem drinker you often have no idea how they will be on a day to day basis.

If at any point in the process of encouraging change your drinker talks about going to the doctor or some other means of getting help, it is important to be encouraging without reminding them that you've heard it all before and that they let you and themselves down on previous occasions. Be calm, listen and say something like "that sounds like a good idea, when do you think you'll call them/go to see them, would you like me to come with you?" Whatever is appropriate and feels comfortable and natural for you to say without being too specific and making the drinker feel under pressure. You may want to practice what you want to say before actually saying it just to check whether you feel you are using the right words and not saying it in a confrontational or cynical way.

Whether people are able to achieve positive change or not can depend on many factors. Timing is very important; if you have reached a point where you feel you cannot continue as you are then it will potentially provide the motivation for change. Some people find change easier than others and may welcome it whilst others are scared of change and see it as delving into the unknown. It could happen due to a friend, family member or doctor noticing that something is wrong and offering to help and talk things through. The initial reaction of the person you talk to can have far reaching effects as if the partner is told that they are making too much of their drinkers behaviour or is made to feel that they should get on with dealing with the circumstances as they have put themselves in that situation, then they are unlikely to consider changing anything.

Once the process of change has commenced some people will find it easy to continue on their new path whilst others may relapse back into old patterns after short or long periods of time. After positive changes have been made, partners need the continued support of people around them to help make sure they don't revert back to old behaviours. People around you may be resistant to allowing you to change if they feel that you are doing what they ought to be doing themselves. For instance, someone in an unhappy marriage may not offer encouragement and support as it will force them to look at their own situation that they may have accepted due to their own fears surrounding change.

Some believe that adapting to change becomes more difficult as you get older whilst others say that they find it liberating as they get older and care less about what people might think or say about them.

The key to change can be to take small steps that gradually bring a large result. The habits that we have become accustomed to need to be relearned and new ones implemented. If you are reading this book as someone who is supporting another person who is living with a drinker then it is important to remember that everyone moves, shifts and changes at different rates depending on what they are comfortable with. Avoid becoming frustrated with them if you feel they should be making changes faster or they appear to be relapsing back into old patterns. Be as supportive and patient as you can whilst reminding them gently of their original goals and intentions.

You might decide to do one or several of the following to help you feel supported during the process of change:

1. Tell someone that you know and feel you can trust with sharing your situation.

2. Ask your doctor or another health professional for help.

3. Do an internet search for support groups and call them or go to a meeting.

4. Phone a helpline to talk to someone who understands your experience.

5. Re-read section 2 and the stories in section 3 of this book so you have some understanding of alcohol dependency and realise you are not the only person going through it.

If you continue doing what you are doing then you will get the same result, the only way to change the result is to change your own behaviour. The first step is to put aside any feelings of shame, guilt or anger with yourself and focus your energy on what small steps you can take. It is important for you to realise that you have choices and do not deserve to be treated badly, whatever your drinker has told you. Every one of us has the right to be treated with respect; you deserve to be happy and to enjoy your life. Believing this can be difficult if you have been told for years that you deserve to be verbally or physically abused. Tell yourself either in your head or out loud and in the present tense "I deserve to be treated well; I deserve to enjoy my life". There may be something else that you feel is more appropriate, use whatever words feel right in your circumstances.

You are the only one who can decide that you want to start taking steps to change your life. It is easy to do and it is easy not to do. You can always find "reasons" or excuses not to do anything and allow things to remain as they are.

Chapter 21: The 7 Stages to achieving change

Stage 1: Review your life

Most people underestimate the hidden strength and courage that they have within them and have forgotten all they have achieved in their lives. If you think back over your life, take some time to review all your achievements. These can be simple things such as academic qualifications, passing your driving test and more life changing events such as having children, job promotion, travelling or whatever is important to you and has made a difference to your life.

We are all good at self-criticism but rarely take the time to remind ourselves of what we are good at or remember all that we have achieved. It does take some effort not to start contradicting the positive thoughts and memories with any negative ones. Take some time to do that now and see how you feel more positive about yourself.

You may find that you start hearing negative voices in your head that want to contradict the positive thoughts. Be aware of them and put them to one side without telling yourself off which is another way of being negative towards yourself. If you start to make negative comments in your head then some people find it useful to literally tell themselves to stop. Others think of seeing the words of the negative thoughts on a computer screen and pressing the delete button so the words disappear or on a blackboard which they can rub out. You could imagine the words going up into the sky, whatever works for you. Start trying out different ways and find out what is most successful for you.

Fundamental to you being able to cope and deal with any potential changes is for you to feel good about yourself and what the future holds. Sometimes we think it is another person that makes us happy when the truth is that we have to make the decision to be happy and experience positive feelings in all areas of our lives. We have a choice as to whether we allow events and circumstance to dictate how we live our lives. Do you believe that you have any control over your life, even only in certain areas or do you believe that everything that happens to us is due to fate and there is nothing we can do to make changes?

If you think back to a time before alcohol began to affect your life, can you recall how you felt about your future, what plans and dreams you had? It is important to dream and look forward to the future; it can help us to deal with the day to day hum drum, difficult or boring things in life. Our dreams are very often reduced or removed altogether when alcohol starts to seriously affect the relationship. Dreams are very personal and can be related to all areas of our lives, most often to financial gain or acquisitions. Alcohol costs and a serious drinker can consume a lot of money which will have a knock on effect as to how much money is left after day to day expenses have been paid. Take some time to write down the things that are important to you and the dreams you would like to have even if they seem totally unobtainable in your current situation. This will enable you to measure how alcohol has affected this part of your life.

You may want to assess your current situation in stages and look at different areas at different times. Do whatever is comfortable for you and in the time you have available. What is important is that you set yourself a date for when you will complete your assessment and that you persevere rather than start and then leave it. Change will happen when you alter your behaviour and the sooner you assess the situation and decide what changes you can make, the sooner there is hope that your circumstances will also change.

Stage 1 Actions:

A. Write down all that you have achieved in your life so far. Whether they are large or small achievements, whatever has had a positive impact on your life and whatever you are proud of or other people have told you they admire you for.

B. Write down any dreams you have and what you would like to have or achieve in the future.

Stage 2: Look after yourself

When we are tired or our health is run down then we find it harder to cope with difficult or challenging situations. One of the first basic stages to change is to start looking after your own body and mind. If you're tired what can you do to make sure that you get more sleep? If you have to remove yourself from your drinking partner and are able to safely do so without leaving anyone else in a dangerous situation then this will give you a chance to gain some clarity and start to develop a sense of self again.

When people become carers or protectors of others then they gradually start to spend more of their time and energy on those that they perceive as needing it rather than themselves. This is particularly prevalent in women who are usually the parent that spends more time with any children or dependant relatives. Learning to think about yourself can be difficult after a long period of selflessness but it is important to realise that you deserve to have time and energy spent on yourself.

Allowing some time in your daily schedule to go for a walk, exercise or spend time outside will have a huge effect on your mental wellbeing. It is well proven that exercise has essential and positive effects on hormones and chemicals that affect our physical and mental health.

Take some time out of your usual daily routine and find somewhere quiet where you will not be disturbed and carry out this basic breathing exercise which will enable you to learn to relax and experience some calm which you may not have experienced for some time. Make sure you are sitting or lying comfortably and take a deep breath in through your nose whilst counting to 5 in your head; hold your breath for 5 counts and then slowly expel the air through your mouth for 10 counts; hold for 5 counts and then repeat the process.

Initially you may find it hard to breath for the number of counts specified but as you become more relaxed you will find that you can make them last even longer. The beauty of this exercise is that it can be done anywhere – on the bus, at work or as you are going to sleep in bed. Carrying out this after going to bed will bring improvement to your sleep. Ideally you need to do the routine at least 5 times to start to notice how you are relaxing but even a couple of times will make a difference. If you can build it into your daily routine as well as in times of great stress it will become a habit and you will do it automatically.

Carrying out this exercise will allow you to develop some clarity around the choices and opportunities you have to change your situation. Learning to breathe deeply and become relaxed sounds simple but we all forget to do this in times of stress. Over long periods of stress the inability to relax our bodies can create illness or disease which is our minds way of telling us that it needs to stop, slow down and that it wants to change. Start thinking about your own health and noticing how you feel. Look after yourself as there is only one of you!

What is your diet like? Do you feel that you are eating healthily and drinking enough water? This sounds very basic but the fundamentals of having a good diet, enough sleep and exercise are easily neglected when we are busy with a difficult home-life or looking after others. When you feel healthy and good about yourself you will find it far easier to deal with difficult situations and it will help to put things into perspective.

Think about how you can put some time aside for yourself and write down what you would like to achieve in looking after yourself and how you would like to feel. Make a commitment to yourself to carry out the changes you write down which can be very small ones but will gradually build up over time. It is very important that you believe that you can carry them out and that they are achievable. Deciding that you want to spend 2 hours exercising every day is unlikely to be sustainable or even healthy and means that you are setting yourself up for potential failure.

Be as specific as you can about what you are going to do and when and where you are going to do it. Imagine what you will feel like when you have achieved it on a regular basis. This is a plan for long term health not something you will do for a month and then gradually let it gradually fall down your list of priorities. You are the no.1 priority as there are probably a few people who depend on you both in and out of the home and if you don't have your health you will be less able to cope and look after those people and certainly not have any energy left over to start enjoying your life.

You deserve to look after yourself and enjoy your life. Now read that statement again, do you find it difficult to accept that it's true? Write it out in the present tense: I deserve to look after myself and enjoy my life. I am looking after myself and enjoying my life. This statement is called a positive affirmation and whilst you may not believe this to be true at this point in time, if you continue to repeat this to yourself, preferably out aloud at least twice a day, then you will eventually find it easier, start believing it and it will then become a reality. Let it become a habit and find times during your day when you can easily fit it in and remember to do it – such as when you're brushing your teeth. If you decide on this time as being the best then it's probably best to do it in your head rather than out aloud!

Stage 2 Actions:

A. Write down what your plan is to improve your health and fitness. What will you do and how will you do it? What will the benefits be when you start carrying out your plans on a regular basis?

B. Write down a positive affirmation statement and put it somewhere that is easily accessible so that you can read it at least twice a day.

C. Practice the breathing exercise as many times during the day as you want or need to.

Stage 3: How you feel about your drinker

Many partners say that the way their problem drinker lies to them is worse than the drinking itself. If the drinker comes home and is clearly drunk but denies having drunk much or any alcohol then the partner will feel that they are unable to trust anything else that the drinker says in other areas of their lives.

The drinker may regard themselves as an honest person and be truthful when sober but the lack of trust that their partner feels towards them can also erode their level of respect for the drinker. Trust and respect are paramount in a personal or business relationship; therefore this can affect relationships in all areas of a drinker's life. The lies that a drinker tells in relation to how much they have had to drink are usually in order to cover up their actual consumption and avoid feelings of guilt and shame, rather than wanting to deliberately mislead their partner.

Often people with a propensity towards inflicting physical or mental abuse will manoeuvre themselves into a firm position in a relationship before the partner is aware that there may be a problem with drinking and their associated behaviour. They will either be living with or get married to someone as fast as possible before the partner discovers that they are a problem drinker. They may do this subconsciously but by having a whirlwind romance it means the length of time that they have to conceal parts of their personality is kept to a minimum. As human beings we want to be loved and if someone is paying you a great deal of attention and making you feel loved and secure then it is an easy trap to fall into.

Over a period of time it is easy to see negative changes in behaviour as temporary or to provide reasons or excuses for the changes. Unless there is someone outside the relationship who is aware of and sees the changes, voices their concerns and is heard then we can become used to them and gradually accept them as being "normal". The old phrase "love is blind" works in these situations where we are convinced that what we are feeling and experiencing is genuine love. In many cases it is and the drinker may not be aware of what they are doing. Their need for love may drive them towards an end goal of settling down as being the catalyst they need to change their drinking habits or they may be unaware that they are a problem drinker.

Confrontation and questions that a drinker perceives as being critical of their behaviour will be met with avoidance and resistance. The drinker thinks of alcohol as their ally or protection rather than a negative influence. If a partner feels the need to pursue questioning in order to prove the drinker has lied then they will potentially invest a great deal of time and emotional effort that will be wasted and unproductive. The drinker is likely to become more defensive and the result will be that the partner feels even more frustrated and angry at the drinker's behaviour. It is unlikely to achieve any change, even if the drinker does admit they have been drinking or had more than they first admitted. It will create further feelings of guilt in the drinker that may result in further drinking rather than a reduction.

Having a conversation with a sober drinker about their drinking can result in total denial that a problem exists. This again lies in the drinker's belief that alcohol is their ally rather than enemy or they may genuinely believe that they do not have a problem. It is not until the drinker becomes aware that the negative effects of drinking outweigh the perceived positive effects that they start to think about changing their behaviour. If the partner continuously covers up for the drinker and clears away evidence of drinking such as empty cans or bottles then the drinker will not be reminded of their behaviour when they were drunk. If there are children in the home then they obviously need to be protected from harm and distress but if possible then leave the empties where they are. If it is possible to leave the drinker where they have fallen asleep rather than getting them to bed, this again may force the drinker to recollect the events that led them to that position.

Some partners will question themselves and wonder how their drinker can behave the way they do if they truly loved them. There may also be a deep fear that if they push them too hard to change their behaviour then the drinker may walk out of the home and leave. However dysfunctional a relationship may be, they may fear being alone more than handling the day to day uncertainty that the drinker brings to their life.

If someone is hurting us either mentally or physically then our survival instinct is to pay them back or punish them for what they have done. Punishment can take various forms and is most commonly inflicted by withholding sex or affection, refusing to look at the drinker or be near the drinker, refusing to have a conversation or carry out household tasks such as cleaning or cooking. The partner may spend more time away from the home and the drinker with an intention of giving the drinker time to consider their behaviour and to hopefully decide to change.

The reality is that if the partner decides to carry out any of the above the drinker may decide to spend the additional time alone drinking and not care if they eat or if the house is clean. The result is that the partner feels more frustrated and powerless, particularly if they continue to use punishment as a reaction to the drinkers more extreme behaviour. The drinker may initially feel some guilt and shame but will quickly recognise the pattern and know that ultimately the partner will revert to "normal" behaviour after a period of time and the actions intended as punishment will have no effect at all.

Another natural reaction is for the partner to become angry and either to express this through shouting or writing angry texts, emails or letters. The anger may have been increasing over a period of time and a final straw can result in a show down that is likely to be full of emotion and cover incidents going back over a period of time. If the drinker is unable to remember the incidents or feels that they are being unjustly accused then they may see the partner as being unreasonable and getting on at them again. The drinker may initially feel guilt or shame but this can lead either to further drinking or becoming numbed to the anger and ignoring it, waiting for it to pass.

Alternatively it can become a full blown shouting match with the drinker feeling that they have to defend themselves and prove to the partner that they are the one who is being unreasonable. The result is further anger and frustration for the partner and again results in a feeling of powerlessness and futility. If the partner had hoped for an apology and a change in the drinker's behaviour then the drinker leaving the house to go and drink more, saying they are misunderstood and that the partner is totally unreasonable is not the desired result. Some drinkers will instigate and encourage an argument or fight in order to have the reason or excuse to leave the situation and drink.

Some partners will try pleading with their drinker, allowing them to see how upset they are without shouting. The result is that again the drinker may have initial feelings of guilt and shame, make apologies and give promises of changing. If the partner pleads with the drinker on a regular basis then eventually the drinker will learn what they need to do to placate the partner and end the pleading session as quickly as possible without them feeling any real shame.

The drinker may already experience a high level of guilt and this may be one of the main reasons they drink so much – in order to numb the negative feelings. The drinker does not necessarily mean to inflict hurt on the partner but they are hurting within themselves and see alcohol as the solution. The drinker's self-esteem is likely to be low and being told that they are not being the partner they used to be or promised to be will make them feel even worse and potentially reinforce the negative spiral so that they experience lower self-esteem and become more defensive.

All of the above reactions are very natural and unfortunately they are unlikely to have the positive effect that the partner would like or hopes for. If you look back over past events and evaluate which of these reactions you have used and the results, were they effective for you? Did you achieve the resultant change that you had hoped for? We are all individuals and although there are certain similarities in a drinker's patterns of behaviour, it is unfortunately not possible to prescribe a solution. Many partners wish that they could tell someone this is the quantity, when and where the drinker drinks and be told they need to carry out x, y and z to achieve a complete change in their drinker's behaviour to bring about a loving, harmonious relationship and home environment.

However, you are not powerless and there are strategies that you can adopt that will assist you in bringing about change. You are the catalyst and the one that has the power to make an assessment of the situation and implement changes that will have a knock-on effect on the drinker in your life. This is contradictory to the twelve steps that Al-anon use in their programme to help partners cope with their problem drinker. Their first step is that you are powerless over alcohol and whilst this may initially give someone comfort and feel that it is not their problem or responsibility, it will also lead them to eventually feeling they have no control over that part of their life. Deciding you are powerless can be releasing on the one hand but debilitating on the other.

External events do affect a drinker's behaviour and once you are able to stand back and analyse these then you may have an influence on their drinking. This could be after you and your partner feel closer or when something happens to make the drinker feel better about themselves. The question is, how did your behaviour change in these circumstances? When we are happy or contented then we naturally view our world and our circumstances in a different way to when we are stressed and feeling low. We will react differently depending on the situation we are in and the people that we are with. Your drinker's behaviour has changed your behaviour and you have the potential to reverse this and change your own behaviour in order to change the drinker's behaviour.

Everything works in circles or spirals and you have the opportunity to stop the downward spiral and change the direction so that it starts to go upwards again and see improvement. If you think about how you felt when you first met your partner, what you were like and what you liked about them, how has that changed? If you look back and remember how you felt and hear some of the things that you used to say to each other, how does that make you feel? Depending on the length of time you have been in your current situation and how long the drinker has been drinking will affect how you view the past and whether you feel there is any hope for the future.

You may be at a point where you feel nothing for the drinker in terms of love and affection, do not trust or respect them and are even disgusted by them. You may have already decided that you have had enough and do not want to be in a relationship with them anymore. If this is the case then this section of the book will reinforce that belief and assist you in making changes that enable you to become more confident and start you on the path of recovery from living with an alcohol dependant partner. This is a personal decision and it is unlikely that people outside the situation will be able to fully appreciate what you have been through and may criticise you for leaving the relationship.

It is important to have some professional or personal support from someone who does have an understanding. There is no need to feel guilty or feel that you have failed in not sustaining the relationship or seeing it through to the bitter end. How and in what manner you extricate yourself from the relationship may affect what influence you ultimately have on your drinker. If he is the father of your children then the long term influence on them may be your motivation for reading this next section on communicating with the drinker in an effective way.

People become depressed when they believe that they have lost control over a part of their lives and they feel helpless or powerless. It is likely that you have realised that you cannot change the drinker's behaviour by talking, shouting, writing, ignoring or any other reaction. Telling other people about the drinker's behaviour and asking them to communicate their opinion to the drinker is also unlikely to be effective.

If on the other hand you absolutely believe there is hope for the relationship and want to do what you can to assist the drinker to get to the point that they want to change, then this section of the book will enable you to improve your own sense of self-esteem. It will give you the tools you need to start the process to implement change and provide the chance to rebuild and improve your relationship.

It is natural that the partner will want the drinker to drink less and they start to keep an eye on how much their partner is drinking. If they are in a social environment the partner may keep a count of how many drinks the drinker has. However, they may not see the reality as a visit to the toilets or to go for a cigarette allows the drinker the opportunity to surreptitiously have additional drinks without being seen. A drinker who says they have had a couple of pints may have had many more but be so used to the effects of alcohol that they are able to hide their actual consumption.

You may feel that even though you have tried talking to your drinker about reducing their alcohol intake and changing their drinking patterns, they haven't done so because you have not used the right words or said it in the right way. The reality is that it doesn't matter what you say or how you say it as it is unlikely to result in change. If you keep on doing what you are doing you will get the same results. The answer is to accept the things that you are unable to change and put your focus on the things that you are able to change. By following these stages you will see the most positive and hopefully productive way of communicating with your drinker.

Stage 3 Actions:

A. Take some time to write about how you first met your drinker and what attracted you to them.

B. Write about when they are more relaxed and seem happier - what were the causes or triggers that resulted in them being in a better mood?

C. What changes can you make to help your drinker become more aware of their behaviour?

D. Write about the areas of your life that have been affected by alcohol.

Stage 4: Look at your life

Plan some time to yourself when you will have the chance to be alone and be able to think for about an hour, when you are unlikely to be disturbed or distracted. Think about the different areas in your life and divide them into these 5 categories:

1.   Relationship with your drinker.

2.   Relationships with family and friends.

3.   Your health.

4.   Work/career.

5.   Finances.

You may have other categories that you would like to add to the list and feel free to add those as long as the list does not become too long. Take some time to assess the current situation in each of the categories and record what is happening in those different areas – you have already looked at your health and your relationship with your drinker so those can be easily redressed. On a scale of 1 to 20, 20 being that you feel really good about them and 1 being you feel very unhappy with things, take some time to give each of the 5 areas a score of how you feel things stand at this time.

It is important to be as objective as possible and look at your life as though you were someone from outside the situation, removing as much emotion as you can and recording the facts. By giving each area a score you can come back to the areas on a fortnightly or monthly basis and reassess them. This gives you a means of measuring whether you feel any improvements have been made.

One of the most painful areas of the assessment can be when you look at how relationships in the household have changed through your drinker drinking heavily. If you think back to how your relationship was and how the drinker has changed, what impact has that had on you and any other people in the home? How does your drinker relate to other family members outside the home and how has drinking affected their friendships on a personal and work level?

Allow yourself to write about any other areas of your life that you feel have been affected by heavy drinking without worrying about how you are writing or whether anyone else will read it or understand why you are affected. You may find that looking at your situation raises negative emotions to the surface that have been deeply buried for a long time. Whatever your reaction is to doing this exercise is the right reaction for you, nobody is judging you. If you leave it and come back to it then you may find that you have a totally different reaction.

Depending on your character, you may have been functioning or existing in survival mode for a long time and not allowed yourself to acknowledge how much the drinking has affected you. On the other hand if the problem has been there a long time and you have had a chance to look at it either on your own or by talking to someone then your reaction may be less strong.

Find somewhere safe that you can put the papers or book in which you are recording in order that you can review the results at a later date. The next stage is to imagine how you would like these areas of your life to be in the future. Just write whatever comes into your mind, however ridiculous and unobtainable it may seem to be at this moment in time. No one is going to read what you have written so you can feel safe to write exactly what you want without fear of being judged. The ideal is to have short term goals – for the coming week, medium term goals for the coming month and long term goals for the coming year. If you find it hard to think too far ahead then you can do it for just one month ahead. Alternatively some people find it easier to think in terms of a year.

Focus is a very powerful thing to do as what we focus on invariably becomes reality. If you focus on all the things that you cannot change then you will feel helpless and be unlikely to find the motivation for change. On the other hand if you focus on what you would like to happen and how you would like things to be then your subconscious mind will work on making those things happen.

Look at the list or words you have written about how you would like your life to be and think about how you will feel when those things happen, what will you see or hear. You can close your eyes and imagine it even more clearly now as you take a few minutes to think positively about how your life could be and what is most important to you.

Stage 4 Actions:

A. Take some time to assess the current situation in each of the 5 categories and record what is happening at the moment in those different areas.

B. Give each of the areas a mark from 1 to 20.

C. Take some time to imagine and write down how you would like these 5 areas of your life to be in the future:

Short term goals:

Medium term goals:

Long term goals:

Stage 5: Let go

Now go back to the 5 areas from stage 4 and think about what could realistically be changed at the moment in each of the 5 areas? What could you do in order to make small changes immediately, today that would have a positive effect on your situation and enable you to see that your actions are having an impact?

Some people find it helpful to make decisions about what they are going to do and assess the situation again after a week, fortnight or a maximum of a month. By re-evaluating your situation and deciding on further small changes you can begin to start building on previous changes and build momentum. This will enable you to see and feel that you have some control over your life and that you are far from helpless. The hardest part is to get going and make the first move as it may seem too enormous a task. Start with tiny steps, small changes that you know you can make. Like a large weight, once it starts moving, make sure you keep it moving. An object in motion is far easier to keep moving than allowing it to stop and then having to expend a large amount of effort to get it moving again.

If you find that something is working and having a positive effect then keep on doing it. If it's not working then you can re-evaluate it and think of other actions that you can take and see what results they give you. Writing everything down is crucial in helping you evaluate and also reminding yourself of the progress you have made. Over a period of time you can look back and see things more clearly and remember to acknowledge that you are responsible for the improvements.

You are focusing on yourself and ways that you can make positive changes. Concentrate on ways of making your home and family a happier and safer place that is somewhere you want to be rather than get away from. Focusing on yourself is not a selfish act; you need to become stronger and happier in order to cause a shift towards change in those around you. If you have children then they will obviously benefit from you becoming more relaxed and having energy and time to devote to them.

When you think about your drinker and their drinking habits it is important to think about ways of reducing the harm from alcohol and not focus on ways of reducing the drinker's alcohol intake. You are going to focus on ways of controlling the results or consequences of drinking as opposed to controlling the drinking itself. This is particularly important if your drinker has been drinking for many years and the habits and behaviours are firmly embedded. If your drinker has not been drinking heavily for a long period of time then in theory it will not take as long for them to accept a change in their behaviour.

There is a well-known concept that a drinker will only change their behaviour once they have reached "rock bottom" and because we are all unique individuals this can mean very different things to each person. The classic picture of a drinker reaching "rock bottom" is of a drunk sleeping on a bench who has lost their home, family, work etc. But "rock bottom" for someone can be feeling that people close to them are losing respect for them and they realise that they are also losing respect for themselves. As human beings we tend to care about what people think of us and will conform to social expectations that we perceive are expected of us. Reaching "rock bottom" could also be triggered by the drinker's health deteriorating or having a health scare that forces them to confront reality.

People change because they either want to avoid pain or because they want to experience more pleasure and get something that they want. The avoidance of pain is usually a stronger motivator than the pursuance of pleasure but both of these natural instincts will assist you in creating change.

The first thing you need to consider is how you can change your current behaviour towards your drinker. How do you react towards them when they have been drinking and what do you do to "look after" them or cover up their drinking? Write down all the things that you do for them due to their drinking from the moment that you get up in the morning until you go to bed. What often happens over time is that the relationship of partners changes to adult and child. Whilst you may have had the best intentions in "looking after" your drinker, you have become the sensible one that takes responsibility for your "child".

If you have been shielding your drinker from the negative effects of alcohol and their drinking then it is now time to stop. They need to experience the effects of drinking heavily and if they wake up on the floor rather than in bed or amongst the debris of the previous night's drinking then that is when they will become more aware of what they are doing. In order to change the balance in the relationship you need to let go and let the drinker start to take responsibility for themselves.

When you review the list that you have made, how many of these can you stop doing without putting yourself, your drinker or anyone else in the household at risk in terms of safety? Write a new list of all the things that you can let go of which will liberate your time and energy and most importantly your focus away from the drinking behaviour. Give this list whatever title you want and re-read it when you have finished to ensure that you have included everything that you can.

You need to include not checking on how much your drinker is drinking, not looking for empties that have been hidden, not keeping count on how much they are drinking. This is a really important part of you letting go and if you find yourself thinking about it as it may have become habitual then you can tell yourself in your head or out loud one of the following positive affirmations or any others that you can think of that work for you and help you to let go and do what you need to do:

> I am not responsible for him/her.
> I am letting go.

It is their choice.
I am not responsible for them.
I am not their parent.
I am free and there is no need to worry.

Remember to write the affirmations out and read them to yourself at least twice a day. Have them with you on a piece of folded paper or somewhere easily accessible if you need to quickly read them and remind yourself.

Some people have found it difficult to imagine actually carrying some of the suggestions out such as not clearing up all the empty bottles or cans after your drinker has left them. If you feel it advisable then you can talk through what you are doing with other members of the household. What is important is that the drinker is unaware of all the changes that you are intending to make. If they were aware they might view it as a passing phase that you will tire of and then things will go back to "normal". If there is someone that you can discuss your plans with who is outside the household then this can be helpful in terms of you feeling that you have some support and the opportunity to off-load and discuss how things are progressing. Encourage them to remind you if you start to go back to previous patterns of monitoring alcohol intake or attempting to reduce your drinker's consumption. You need to accept that this will take time and is not likely to result in instant changes in your drinker.

If you have been tip-toeing around the morning after a drinking session in order that you avoid waking them, there is no need to do that. Rather than being anxious that noise created by you or any children will disturb them if the drinker didn't get to sleep until the early hours, let them experience what lack of sleep feels like. If they get into bed and leave clothes or belongings around, leave them. If they come home late and miss dinner then give the food away, freeze it or dispose of it. A drinker often behaves like a young child and as long as you are shielding them then they are unlikely to take any responsibility for their behaviour or even consider changing it.

You can start to spend your time on yourself rather than watching or protecting your drinker. The time that you have spent clearing up after them or anxiously hovering to see what they are doing and how much they are drinking can be spent in other ways that will take you out of the situation and help you to start focusing on yourself and your needs.

If you have been avoiding seeing friends or family because of the drinker's behaviour then start to see them again and open up to the people that you feel you can trust. Perhaps you have always wanted to spend time learning something new, changing your job, doing voluntary work, taking the children somewhere, whatever it might be, if it's important to you and will make you feel good and start to enjoy your life more, then do it!

Some experts say that you should not cover up or make excuses if your drinker is unable to work due to the effects of alcohol. This may not be practical if you are reliant on their income. You do need to be practical, there is no point in making your personal situation worse as this may simply give the drinker another "reason" to drink. I have met several people whose drinkers lost their jobs and sunk even further into the cycle of drinking more and for longer periods. It caused the partners further frustration and anger as their drinkers made little or no effort to find new work and they became more reliant on their partners to support them financially and emotionally.

You may find it difficult to imagine changing your behaviour in the way I have described and being able to think about yourself rather than your drinker. Some people feel guilty as though they are doing something wrong. This is a perfectly normal reaction if you have been living this way for a long period of time. There is absolutely no need to feel guilty and it is important to remind yourself that the drinker is doing what they are doing out of their choice. You are not forcing them to drink and whatever caused them to start drinking heavily in the first place is not a reason for them to have continued drinking. They have chosen to drink at this time even if they appear to be completely out of control.

If the drinker is in physical danger or if they are putting your own or others' lives in danger then this takes precedent over anything. Make sure that all the people involved in your family unit are safe and that no one will suffer long term damage.

Stage 5 Actions:

A. Write down what you could do in order to make some small changes immediately that may have a positive effect on the situation.

B. Plan how and when you will implement these changes either today or in the very near future.

C. What would you like to do for yourself to make you feel better?

D. Write out the positive affirmations that will remind you to let go.

Stage 6: Positive experiences

So by leaving the drinker to experience the negative effects of alcohol they will start to experience some pain. In order for them to be motivated to change their behaviour there also ideally needs to be some pleasure, or an experience of the positive effects of not drinking. This may seem like a strange thing for you to be considering after all the things your drinker has done and when you feel perhaps that they deserve to be punished rather than rewarded. Again, if you consider the analogy of dealing with a child, you will find it much easier to get a child to do something if they feel there is a treat or something advantageous at the end. As human beings we find it easier to be motivated by pleasure and the thought of doing something that we want to do rather than avoiding pain and something unpleasant. As mentioned earlier we tend to spend more effort in avoiding pain but the combination of the two is ideal.

If you think back to when you first met and got to know your drinker you may well be able to remember things that you both enjoyed doing together. Circumstances change over time and there may be other constraints such as finances or young children but you are likely to be able to think of something that you could do together when your drinker is sober. You need to think of something that you would both enjoy as it needs to give you both pleasure. If you suggested something that you wouldn't really enjoy then you will be spending time on your drinker's behalf rather than for your joint benefit. It is best to avoid suggesting something that could be associated with drinking or at a time of day when they start drinking. If you can think of something that occurs earlier in the day then over time once you have both experienced some positive experiences it will be easier to gradually suggest other things that occur later in the day.

The idea is that your drinker needs to be sober and see this positive experience as an alternative to drinking. If they start drinking first thing in the morning then this is obviously more difficult as it will require asking the drinker to refrain from drinking. When you make a suggestion to spend time together when they haven't been drinking then it needs to be done in a non-confrontational way. If you can choose a moment to make a suggestion when the drinker is sober and when you are relaxed then it will be easier for them to consider the idea without perceiving it as an ultimatum.

One of the main reasons for having time together is to encourage a sense of closeness to develop or to be rekindled. In order to cope with their drinking and associated behaviour such as lying, lack of dependability etc. you may have become distant in an attempt to protect yourself from being hurt further. With a child that behaves badly you would normally offer a reward for good behaviour after their behaviour had improved, so offering your drinker a reward in order to encourage change may seem as though it's back to front.

If you have tried everything else without success, then why not give this a go, what have you got to lose? You may enjoy yourself which is fundamental to your drinker relaxing and feeling able to enjoy themselves as well. Put simply, what you are doing is demonstrating to your drinker that they can have more fun, moments of happiness and joy by spending time with you rather than a bottle of alcohol! You are making them aware that they have choices; they can decide how they want to spend their time and ultimately whether they choose to spend their time drinking.

The next part may be hard for you and will require some work. Over a period of time you have experienced anger, frustration, fear, dislike or even feelings of hatred towards your drinker and in order for time together to be pleasant you need to let these go as they will do you no good. I am not suggesting that it is easy or necessary to forgive all that you feel your drinker has done to you but unless you can let it go then it will be a barrier to moving forward. It is important to retain a sense of realism and not expect miracles after one experience of positive time together. You may have been hurt and disappointed many times and this may harden you against the idea and prevent you from allowing yourself to feel positive feelings towards your drinker. There are several ways this can be done and I would suggest you read through them and decide which one would most appeal to you or think of your own variation.

1. You can imagine putting all the negative feelings and memories away in a box and up on a shelf with the lid firmly on.

2. Write down all the feelings of resentment, regrets and times that you felt rejected, in a book and put it somewhere safe so you can add to it another time and bring the negative feelings out of you.

3. Write down all the feelings of resentment, regrets and times that you felt rejected on a piece of paper and burn it somewhere safely, watching the smoke rise up into the sky and telling yourself "I let these feelings go" or whatever wording is appropriate for you.

Just do whatever works well for you and if it doesn't work then do something else until you get the result that you want. If you approach someone when you are relaxed and smiling naturally, then you will get a very different response than if you are tense and have a worried or stressed look on your face. If you walk down the street smiling, whilst some people might wonder why you are smiling, they are very likely to return your smile naturally.

When we smile and laugh we produce natural endorphins that basically make us feel good so if you can start to make an effort to smile or even laugh it will have a positive effect on you. Laughter, even if it is forced and faked is a great de-stresser, next time you are on your own in the car or somewhere that you won't be observed or heard just take a deep breath in and force yourself to laugh even if you don't think you have anything to laugh about! If you continue to do this for about 5 minutes you will be amazed at the effect that it will have on you. You may feel light headed from taking deep breathes and laughing for as long as you can before running out of breath. What you will find is that you feel more relaxed and calmer afterwards.

Take some time to remember your relationship when you first met and the sort of things you did together, what you talked about that made you both laugh. This may give you some ideas for suggesting something similar that you could both do together. Laughter between people in a relationship is very powerful in creating a bond.

It will take more than one positive experience of spending time together to result in the drinker beginning to understand how a change in their behaviour could result in a change in their home life and other areas. You may feel that you want to put a time limit on how long you give your drinker to make even a small change. I would recommend that you take some time to review the situation on at least a monthly basis in order that you can assess the situation and be aware of any improvements as this will provide you with the motivation to continue and the encouragement that you need.

By letting your drinker have the two experiences of seeing the negative effects of drinking and the positive effects of not drinking it will be stronger than just doing one or the other. Taking time to make plans for future experiences that you can both look forward to helps you both to start dreaming again and create a future together. You may find yourself thinking about small things that you can do to the home environment that will make it feel different. Even just painting a room a different colour can change the mood of a room dramatically.

Think of small and easily achieved projects that you and your drinker can do either separately or together that will gradually create a better environment for everyone in the household. These projects need to be small in order that the drinker feels that they are capable of completing them without it becoming an area of stress and disappointment if they are not completed. Remember that even if your drinker appears to be controlling or verbally abusive when they have had too much to drink, the reason for this is very often due to lack of self-esteem and their desire to ensure that you also have low self-esteem so that you stay with them.

Remind yourself that you are a good person and that you deserve to be treated well. Continue to practice the breathing exercise and any of the other exercises in this book that work for you. You are going to need to stay positive and motivated in order that you continue to repeat the positive and negative experiences for some time and retain the belief that change will happen. This does require work from you on a long term basis and you will be surprised at how determined and strong you will become. Change doesn't happen overnight and will take some time but by carrying out a monthly assessment you will be able to see how a shift of a few degrees each month will gather momentum.

Stage 6 Actions:

A. Write down any ideas you may have for doing something that you could both enjoy doing together.

B. Improve your attitude to your drinker by writing down all the feelings of resentment, regrets and times that you felt rejected and get the negative feelings out of you.

C. What can you do to improve your home life?

D. Set yourself some target dates for achieving some evidence of change and record them on a minimum of a monthly basis.

Stage 7: Pulling everything together

Now take some time to review your list of the things that you would like to do together, either the two of you as partners, or as a family or both. These can range from being very simple and short term ideas to longer range and more expensive ideas that may take some time and money to carry out. If you have children and feel it appropriate then you could always ask them what they would like to do and have a few ideas to run past them to make sure that they would also find the ideas enjoyable.

If you have young children and are able to have someone to look after them whilst you spend time with your drinker then this is a huge advantage. Time spent together without the distractions and demands of children will allow you to focus on yourselves and hopefully remind you of what brought you together in earlier years before any pressures of family life were present.

You will find it difficult to follow through with either letting go or spending positive time with your drinker if you are not feeling positive about the potential future you could share together. Due to repeated disappointment and time feeling resentful, rejected, angry and frustrated you will need to work on putting these negative feelings to one side however hard that may seem. Take some time to write a list of the things that first attracted you to your partner and leave aside how your feelings have changed due to their drinking.

Some people find it easier if they give the situation a time limit. This makes them feel that they have a choice in the future as to whether they go back to the original question of whether they stay or leave the relationship. If you feel that you are not able to be committed to making all these changes and are sure that your drinker will let you down again then you will probably be right – it is a self-fulfilling prophesy and what you truly believe and wish for is very likely what you will end up with. Put simply, be sure what you wish for is what you really want. Are you looking at this and thinking about giving it a go so that you will feel less guilty and that you have done what you can to save the relationship and are then able to freely walk away without feeling any guilt?

As humans we can be very good at convincing ourselves that we are feeling a certain way and only later on are we able to look back and realise that we actually felt very differently and were going through the motions due to peer or family pressure. Being honest with yourself at this stage may save you both time and heartache. If you look at yourself and your life at this point in time are you certain that you know what you want or what is best for you?

Once you have made a decision on what changes you want to make then you need to prepare to talk to your drinker. As already described earlier it is important that despite all the history and your negative feelings towards your drinker they are unlikely to listen if your approach is confrontational, angry or you show signs of frustration and resentment. This is an important meeting and if you can explain your ideas and thoughts without any negative emotion then it has the potential to start a shift in their behaviour and lead to the changes you want. You want to communicate your ideas without resulting in an argument or fight. If you go into the meeting feeling that it will be a waste of time and just result in the same outcome then it most likely will. Having a positive frame of mind is crucial.

Take some time to review your notes about what first attracted you to your drinker and what personality or character traits first attracted you to them. If you start a meeting with telling them what you love about them and reminding them of past times together that were positive and loving then it will set a good base for a positive meeting and mean that they avoid feeling defensive as to why you have wanted to talk to them. If your talks usually result in raised voices and an argument then that is what they will be expecting. It is up to you whether you arrange the meeting in advance or pick a time when they appear to be in a good mood and when you think they will be more receptive to listening.

If you find that you do not feel love towards your drinker and are unable to say anything positive about how you currently feel about them then you can talk more about the past without blaming them for the changes that have resulted in a negative effect on your relationship. What is often helpful is to write down what you want to say, whether that be some bullet points or word for word – whatever works best for you. It may seem very calculated to practice either saying it in your head or out loud but it will help to say it more naturally and easily when you actually say it in the meeting.

Then take some time to review what activities you could do with your drinker and decide on a few with some idea of when they might be able to take place. When you ask your drinker to join you for these activities please ensure that you make it clear that they can only take place if your drinker doesn't drink just before or during them. If you plan something and they arrive clearly having had a drink then it is important that you have a plan B that you can go ahead with that removes you from their company and gives them time to think. You can arrange the activity for another time, again making it clear that it will not go ahead if they have been drinking. There are no set formulas for these Stages and it is important for you to decide beforehand if you will go ahead if they appear to have had a drink but not be in a bad state. You can set the boundaries and bear in mind that like a child they may push them just to check how serious you are.

Ensure that any plans they agree to, have a clear start time and then if they do not turn up you give them a little time for running late but then leave and go ahead with your plan B. You may have spent a lot of time waiting for your drinker to arrive in the past and part of turning up on time is having respect for you and valuing your time. Your drinker does have a clear choice as to whether they choose to spend time with you or drink. If they choose drink it is important for you to avoid taking this personally.

Finally take some time to review what you have written about the consequences of their drinking and what areas you are going to let go. This can be very hard to imagine going through with but like many things thinking about it is worse than reality as we often conjure up the worst case scenarios in our minds. If you have been hiding your drinkers drinking habits from friends and family then now is the time to start to speak to those that you feel will be understanding and may be able to provide you with some support.

So now you have the three parts to your meeting:

1. Telling them how you feel about them or past experiences and reasons why you love/loved them.

2. Explaining the things that you will no longer do for your drinker.

3. Suggesting alternatives for spending positive time together, making it clear that you will make plans to do something by yourself if they chose not to join you.

The idea is to start and end with something positive - in coaching this is called the feedback sandwich. It makes it easier for someone to receive and hear what you want to communicate – the middle part or "sandwich filling" without feeling bombarded with criticism and becoming defensive. If you feel that you do not wish to spend time with your drinker then you can use parts 1 and 2 to negotiate an improvement in home life through compromises.

It is important to remember that you are not attempting to reduce their alcohol intake but rather protect yourself from the effects. This involves accepting the level of drinking and asking that they make sure they refrain from actions that could cause danger such as late night cooking when they are very drunk. If you provide a dispassionate explanation for being concerned about your safety and any other people in the household without becoming over emotional or angry then it will have more effect.

If you have children then it would be wise to arrange to have the meeting when they are not around to make sure you are not disturbed. If your drinker has been drinking heavily before the meeting then it is best to leave it until another time as they may not remember what is discussed or may become aggressive. You can use your notes to remind you of what you want to say and the areas that you want to cover. At the beginning of the meeting it is vital to let your drinker know that you are not going to ask them to reduce their drinking or stop altogether. The reason you want to talk to them is to improve the current situation and that you want to work together on achieving that as an outcome or result.

Once you have said how you feel or felt about your drinker then you can give them a chance to say what they think. If they are argumentative or aggressive in response to what you have said then you can decide if you want to proceed with the other parts of the meeting or not. If you are calm and they understand that you do not want to argue then they should relax. If they attempt to draw you into an argument then you need to exit from the situation as you will not achieve anything through argument as you already know.

If you decide to exit then make sure you do so without storming off in anger. Thanking someone for their time and saying "maybe we can talk another time" or "perhaps we can talk again next week" will leave the possibility open for further discussion another time and make sure that you avoid a sense of failure if you haven't covered all the areas that you wanted to.

Their response maybe that they have not changed since you first met and that you are the ones that have changed and caused problems in the relationship. Rather than answer back, become defensive or start an argument you can respond by saying something like "thank you for saying what you feel/think" and then move on. Use whatever words you feel comfortable with, what you are doing is acknowledging what they have said without giving an opinion.

Now you can move onto part 2 of the meeting and explain the areas that you are going to let go and the things that you will no longer carry out. Again your drinker needs to be told in a calm and rational manner without them feeling that they are under attack. When you have finished each area you can ask them what they think and take the time to listen to them so that they feel they have been heard. If they respond positively and you think they may be prepared to find a solution then you can ask them "what do you think we should do?" or "what do you think might be a solution?"

If they react badly or become aggressive then make sure that you do not become involved in a pointless argument. You may want to make notes as to what you are going to say and what has been said. If a statement is misunderstood by your drinker then it's easy to say this is what I said and point to what you have written rather than start arguing. When someone does become defensive then they can easily believe that you have said something that you haven't because their brain is in self-protection mode.

You could also have a written list of the things that you are no longer prepared to do and give this to them so that they have something to refer to and it is as clear as possible.

The words that you use in these discussions are really important. If you tell someone "you make me really angry when you smoke in the house when you're drunk" you will get a very different reaction than if you say "when you smoke in the house when you have been drinking then I feel frightened that you may drop a cigarette and start a fire". The first sentence indicates blame and is accusatory whereas the second sentence expresses how you feel without being aggressive and causing a defensive reaction.

Whilst it is difficult to accept you need to understand that nobody can force you to feel a certain way and you have a choice as to how you react. You can respond by being angry or choosing to ignore the behaviour. Some people are not very good at saying what they really meant to say or what they feel. As the person saying something it is your responsibility to communicate effectively. Their reaction should help you know whether your communication has worked in the way you wanted and intended it to.

Once you have finished the meeting take some time to review what has been said and make any notes that you want on how the meeting went. What worked well and got the most positive response? This will help you when it comes to measuring and evaluating your progress over the coming weeks or months and will help keep you motivated when you are able to see the small steps that result in progress. It may be that change occurs quickly and it is also possible that it will take some time and that you will need to be patient and not feel disappointed if you have to repeat parts of the meeting again before you start to get the results that you are looking for.

Stage 7 Actions:

A. Review notes about what first attracted you to your drinker.

B. Review notes about the consequences of their drinking and what areas you are going to let go.

C. Review what positive experience you would like to have with your drinker.

D. Plan the meeting and think about the language you will use.

E. Review the meeting and make notes for future reference.

Section 5

Chapter 22: Review of the change process

If you are able to take the time to do a weekly review on what changes have occurred this would be helpful. If things start to improve then you could arrange another meeting to discuss further alternatives for spending time together or improving your home life. On the other hand if no change has occurred then you may have to simply repeat certain parts of the meeting, being sure to use the "feedback sandwich" method again. In your review you need to also assess your own behaviour and make sure that you are being less controlling on how much your drinker is drinking and letting go in all the areas that you intended. Remind yourself why you are doing this and of what your long term goals are.

Continue to take time for yourself, gradually building your self-esteem and removing yourself from the pressures of home life. Take time to review your health and make sure that is improving as well. Are you doing all that you promised yourself that you would do? Are you still talking to someone and getting some support? When you are talking to anyone about your drinker it is important not to let it become a ranting and blaming session. This is not about anyone being right or wrong. You do not want judgement to affect how you relate to your drinker as you will need to remain as positive as possible and accept the drinking as it is, rather than continuing to watch and control.

Before starting this process of encouraging change it may be advisable to set a time limit on how long you are prepared to wait and see if there is any change in your drinker. This will help to make you feel that there is an end to uncertainty and make sure that you continue to assess the situation on a weekly and monthly basis so that you are aware of how things are progressing. By writing things down each month it makes it far easier for you to recall what the situation was like and to note down any changes, however small they may seem.

If you set a time limit of 3 months for example and at the end of that time you believe that you have seen no reduction in their drinking, disruptive, aggressive or other negative behaviour, then you need to step back and assess whether there really is no change at all. If there has been no improvement then you need to consider whether you are prepared to give them further time or not.

If change doesn't happen

If you decide that you cannot or do not want to continue then you will know that you have done what you could and that any feelings of guilt and shame are not deserved. It is very common at the end of any type of relationship to feel a sense of failure that it has not worked out but the reality is that your drinker may be a long way off getting to their "rock bottom" and may never even get there. Often the fear of ending the relationship is far worse than dealing with it and starting the process. It could be that the threat of separation will have an impact on your drinker and having a meeting where you calmly explain that you are unable to live this way anymore and need to have a period of time away from the drinker will result in them promising to change.

Again it is important not to raise your hopes too high if promises to change have been given before. If you decide to give them a final chance then it is advisable to set out clearly what changes need to take place and what time limits there are. Writing down what they have agreed they want to change and by when gives very clear boundaries and guidelines for both of you to see and measure whether these are further broken promises or a concerted effort by them to change.

Chapter 23: Stay or leave?

Once you have carried out an assessment and completed all the stages that you want to or feel are appropriate in chapter 20 then you may find it easy to sit back and know what you want to do. On the other hand you may need to leave it for a few days, weeks or months and let things settle down emotionally in order that any negative emotions do not cloud your vision.

It is important not to allow yourself to rationalise the situation to the point that you create inertia and manage to convince yourself that you are powerless to make any decisions: this is not true. You do have choices and you can make decisions. In their simplest form you can decide to do one of the following options:

1. Do nothing.

2. Do something.

Once you have decided whether you choose option 1 or 2 then you can choose one of the following:

If your choice was option 1 then you can finish reading the book or put it aside and read it again when you get to the point where you feel your choice is option 2.

If your choice is option 2 then you can decide which of the following choices are right for you:

A. Leave the relationship.

B. Stay in the relationship and make changes by working through the 6 stages again and/or getting some professional help.

This is over simplification of all the complications of your situation and relationship but essentially this is what it boils down to. What do you want? What would be best for your family? What is best for your future?

If you decide to stay

If you decide that you want to choose option B and stay with your drinker then take some time to sit down again when you know you will be undisturbed and have at least an hour to yourself to think and write.

Re-read all that you have written from stage 1 to 7 and any notes you've made after meetings with your drinker. Review any progress that you think has been made, in which areas and what have been the most successful methods of encouraging change? Decide what you want to continue with and the best method of implementation.

Meeting other people who have similar experiences to your own can help in making you feel less isolated. There may be some self-help groups in your area and certainly Al-anon groups that could provide you with support. Reading the stories in this book will help you realise that unfortunately living with a problem drinker is a common problem and whilst the details and circumstance maybe different there are underlying similarities.

If your drinker does manage to change either on their own or with outside help then it is important that you continue to work on yourself throughout this time. You may have very strong ideas of what their recovery will mean and how your life will be together in the future. It is possible that even if you have shared your thoughts and dreams with your drinker they may not have the same dreams or even feel concerned that they will not live up to them.

Having dreams is important and it is also important to be realistic. You want the relationship to be rekindled and to reinstate the love and affection that was there in the beginning of the relationship but it may not be possible due to what you have experienced during your partner's period of heavy drinking and changes in your lives such as children, reduced finances etc.

On the other hand it is equally important to remain positive that your drinker will stay the course and be able to recover. Due to past repeated disappointments and frustrations this can be hard and the danger is that if you distance yourself and expect them to fail, they will sense this. They may then feel that you are not providing them with the support and encouragement they feel they deserve and need. If they feel you don't care whether they are drinking or not their own resolve may be affected. Yet again you are in a situation where your beliefs and actions may affect the final outcome and only you will know the best course of action and be able to monitor the situation.

It is very important to continue to communicate with each other and you may want to seek outside help and go to counselling or therapy by yourself or as a couple. Once they have stopped drinking it will take time for you to trust that this is a long term change and to be able to relax without worrying that they are going to start drinking again. Living for a long time with a drinker will have changed both of you and it is almost like getting to know each other again. Continuing to spend positive time together and plan small short term goals helps to keep the momentum of change progressing.

The drinker may develop new interests, friends or work and you need to be able to let go of them and leave them free to explore the possibilities these provide. In the same way it is important to share joint interests and time together it is also important to spend time apart pursuing your own interests or goals. You both need time to get to know yourselves as well as each other. Rather than constantly thinking back to the past when you first met and comparing it with the present it is more helpful to see it as a journey that you can travel together.

There are many cases where a drinker goes to AA reluctantly at first and then finds such solace in the meetings that they go on a very regular basis, sometimes even nightly. Some relationships flounder at this point as the partner can feel that they have lost their drinker again only this time to AA. There are also many cases where the newly sober partner meets another ex-drinker and the common bond of having been a problem drinker is strong enough to be the catalyst for a new relationship. This is very painful for the non-drinking partner who feels they have stuck with them through all the hard times and now that they are sober someone else will reap the rewards and have the best time with them.

Others have developed other habits such as getting back into shape and improving their fitness to the point of obsession. Both of these examples could be seen as obsessive behaviour and whilst the partner will be pleased that they are no longer drinking they will need to come to terms with the fact that they are still absent from the home.

If you decide to stay and persevere with your drinker then please consider getting some professional help to ensure that you continue to make progress and look after yourself. You may find it useful to consider a time limit for another review to ensure that things do not drag on and you allow promises of change to be continually broken without any real progress being made.

If you decide to leave

One of the most difficult things to do if you decide on separation is to be able to let go and understand that you are not responsible for your drinker and whatever actions they decide to take. Some partners experience an enormous amount of inner conflict if they see their drinkers going downhill after separation. Sometimes the children will refuse to see the drinking parent as they no longer want the embarrassment, shame or anger associated with that parent. If the children are of an age where they can decide themselves whether they want to have contact with the drinking parent then it is important to let them exercise that right. On the other hand it is important that your feelings of resentment, disappointment or anger do not result in you using the opportunity to express your negative feelings and affect the children's opinion of the drinking parent.

It is well known that even if a parent is incapable of being what is thought of as a good parent, the child will naturally still have very strong feelings for them as a parent and may want some kind of contact as the bond is so strong. Children who have been mentally or physically abused may still want contact with the parent that has abused them. It may be advisable to seek a professional opinion so that the child has controlled access to ensure that their experience of abuse does not continue to impact their lives. It could cause problems in future relationships or enable a cycle of abuse to emerge that means they repeat their experience with their own children.

Relationships are complicated and when one party is unable to fully control their behaviour due to alcohol then it generates further complications. You will need to trust your instincts of the best way to deal with your drinker as you know better than most how they are likely to react in different situations. However, be wary of spending too much time worrying or considering how they will respond as it may prevent you from carrying out the actions that you need to take in order to resolve the situation.

When you let go of feeling responsible for your drinker it will be a huge weight off your shoulders as you now have the time and energy to think about what is best for you and your family. It is important to continue working on yourself to give you the strength and resolve to carry on and get through the separation and divorce. You may find that your drinker will blame their own behaviour on you; it is unlikely that they will take responsibility for the results of their drinking and if they do, it may be short-lived as they develop new drinking habits or return to old ones.

It is quite common for a drinker to try different tactics to attempt to change their partner's mind. They may be cajoling and promising that they really will change this time and change tactic if that doesn't work. Be prepared for a whole armoury – they may be angry and accusatory or show signs of depression and even threaten suicide if you leave. Please remember the occasions when you have heard similar promises and take professional guidance if you feel the drinker's life or your own life is in danger.

You are now able to reconnect with family and friends who were lost whilst you were with your drinker. You are also free to plan what you would like your future to be and that of your family. It is important to come to terms with what has happened in the past and what occurred in your relationship in order that you can learn from anything that you feel was a mistake. If you are able to see some form of therapist to work through any issues that need resolving then this will help make you feel sure that you have learnt the lessons you needed to learn and can move on to eventually form a new relationship in the future. You need to learn and understand so that you know you will not repeat any negative patterns that you have had in the past.

Whatever happens in your relationship, whether it continues or not, the quickest way to move on is to be able to accept that what has happened cannot be changed. The past is over and you need to get to the point where you are able to learn from your experiences and forgive your drinker for what occurred. More importantly you also need to forgive yourself for allowing yourself to become embroiled in the situation and not give yourself a hard time. This also takes time to work through.

Many people will experience a series of emotions over a period of time – similar to the grieving process. You may go through times of feeling anger, resentment, regrets, and sadness for what might have been. You need to question how these feelings will help you and the reality is that they won't. At first you may find yourself thinking about it several times a day, then daily and eventually less and less. This is important as if you focus on the past you will stay in the past and constantly thinking about it will raise the same negative emotions. There is a saying that the point of power is in the present - you are in control of your future.

If there are children in the family then the most practical solution would be to ask your drinker to leave the home. There may be many financial and practical matters to resolve before separation is possible and seeing at least one solicitor to obtain advice is advisable as the decisions and actions you decide upon may impact a separation or divorce. Most solicitors will give a free 30 minute interview to new clients and this gives you the opportunity to meet them, be sure that you trust them and feel you can work with them. If there are children involved then separating on as good terms as possible will help make a more positive foundation for a future relationship as parents of your children.

Unfortunately there are no prescribed formulas and there are no step by step stages that you can simply follow to be assured of as smooth a separation as possible. It is quite likely that there will be a period of time when you experience a great deal of stress but this can be worked through and you will know that eventually things will get better and you will be in control of a future that you can create. Remember that you deserve to be happy and enjoy life, whatever that means to you.

Closing

Thank you for taking the time to read this book, I hope it has been helpful in giving you sufficient information to enable you to feel informed and able to make the decision that is best for you.

Time is the most precious thing that we have. It cannot be regained or negotiated and you need to be sure that you are making the most of your time here on this earth. Never regret your yesterday, life is in you today and you make your tomorrow.

It doesn't matter what other people think - your thoughts and opinions about how you are living your life are most important. I wish you all the best and hope that life brings you all that you wish for and deserve. Take really good care of yourself and remember that you are unique and truly special.

About the Author

Karenna Wilford ran a successful Architectural and Interior Design practice in London until ten years ago. Having gone through a divorce and serious illness which prevented her from working for nine months, she had the opportunity to re-evaluate her life's ambitions and made the decision to change direction in her career path.

Karenna was introduced to Neuro Linguistic Programming (NLP) by a friend and was so fascinated by the subject that she started to read and research, eventually deciding that her aspirations were to become a Personal and Professional coach. In 2006 she became a fully qualified Life Coach, Health and Success Coach, Master practitioner in NLP and a fully trained Hypnotherapist and went on to become a Time Line Therapy and Theta Therapy Practitioner.

Karenna is now divorced with 2 children and has gained personal experience and understanding of the challenges associated with forming new relationships, running a business and raising children. Karenna has herself experienced living with a problem drinker and decided to write this book to help other people in a similar situation. She works with partners of problem drinkers and also with alcohol dependants, both separately or as couples.

Karenna passionately feels that people should have the opportunity to make the most of their lives and not allow time to slip away through accepting unsatisfactory situations. She feels we are on this earth in order to learn, grow and express ourselves in our own unique way.

Karenna is able to work with clients by telephone, Skype or in person, dependant on distance and preference. If you would like to receive professional help, whether as the partner, family member or drinker then please contact Karenna directly via her website: www.karennawilford.co.uk.

Karenna and her son's Leon and Max

10% of the profits generated by the sale of this book are donated to charity.

Contact list

The following contact details are for the United Kingdom. Please carry out an internet search for help local to your location.

Action for Change: www.action-for-change.org

Offering help, support and advice for the drinker and their partners or family members. Provides publications for the drinker to help reduce the harmful effects of alcohol.

Addaction: 020 7251 5860, info@addaction.org.uk

Support for family members, partners and young people affected by drugs and alcohol. Offers a rehabilitation service to beat problems with addiction.

Adfam: 020 7553 7650, www.adfam.org.uk

Supporting families affected by drugs and alcohol. Provides publications for families and details of local family support groups. Adfam works with family members affected by someone else's drug or alcohol use.

Al-Anon Family Groups UK and Eire: 020 7403 0888, www.al-anonuk.org.uk

Helpline providing support for families and friends of problem drinkers, whether the person is still drinking or not.

Alcohol Concern: www.alcoholconcern.org.uk

The website includes an online directory of services local to you.

Alcohol Focus Scotland :www.alcohol-focus-scotland.org.uk

Telephone information, advice and other services for people concerned about their own or someone else's drinking. Details of where to get counselling and support.

Alcoholics Anonymous (AA): 0845 7697 555, www.alcoholics-anonymous.org.uk

Over 3,300 groups in the UK. Help drinkers to stay sober and to help other alcoholics to achieve sobriety.

Drinkline: 0800 917 8282 (England) 0800 7314 314 (Scotland)

Advice and information for people with alcohol problems or anyone concerned about alcohol misuse. Advice on sensible drinking and information on services to help people cut down on their drinking.

National Association for Children of Alcoholics: 0800 358 3456, www.nacoa.org.uk

Helpline offering information, advice and support to children of alcoholics and people concerned about their welfare

SupportLine Telephone Helpline: 01708 765200, email: info@supportline.org.uk

Provides emotional support and details of local helplines, counsellors providing specific help relating to alcohol.